PRAISE FOR *ENVELOPED*

. . . .

"I was hooked from the opening sentence of *Enveloped*—and it just got better from there. This one woman's story is a story for all of us. God can heal all wounds, and Carol reminds us of this as we see her personally move from shock to heartbreak to wholeness and happiness. Please read this book. It is simply lovely."

—Casey Truffo, marriage and family therapist, author, and private practice coach, beawealthytherapist.net

"In *Enveloped*, Dr. Carol Erb provides a powerful combination of personal experience and professional wisdom. Carol lived it, so she gets it. She will help you get through your crisis and live the life God has planned for you."

—Dr. David Clarke, Christian psychologist, speaker, and author of *I Don't Love You Anymore*, davidclarkeseminars.com

"What can be worse than discovering your spouse has been unfaithful? It leaves you feeling alone, helpless, and hopeless. Proverbs 13:12 says, 'Hope deferred makes the heart sick.' That is a terrible place to be. Carol Erb's book, *Enveloped*, brings hope to those who are heartsick because of the pain of betrayal. This book is warm, heartwrenching, and enlightening. She tells how the betrayal of 'marital love' brought her to her 'True Love,' Jesus Christ. I highly recommend it to anyone who has gone through the despair of divorce."

—Tempe Brown, author, speaker, and Stonecroft Ministries –SC regional speaker/trainer, tempebrown.com

"Carol Erb's *Enveloped* is a truly inspiring story that displays the strength that each of us has inside ourselves. I love that even through all the heartache and betrayal, Carol shows us it's possible to trust again and move forward to find love, joy, and fulfillment. She reminds us that there is a true love out there waiting for everyone, a never-ending love."

—Chelsea Berler, author and speaker, mostlychelsea.com

"Dr. Carol Erb shares her journey from betrayed spouse to Christian counselor and marriage coach. *Enveloped* is a beautiful memoir sharing how God took one woman's experience of loss, death, and betrayal and created help, hope, and goodness. If you or your clients have experienced betrayal and are trying to find God's way through the pain, I'd highly recommend this book."

—Miranda Palmer, marriage and family therapist
and private practice coach, zynnyme.com

"*Enveloped* is the compelling story of a young wife and mother whose serene life was rocked by betrayal and abandonment. While the book is a must-read for women facing marital trauma or divorce, it is also a valuable read for men. I believe if some men who abandoned their wives and kids had read this riveting account of Carol's life before deciding to leave their families, they may have made different choices."

—Baxter Ennis, CEO, Ennis Media Group,
(Lt. Colonel, United States Army–Retired)

"*Enveloped* is a book of encouragement. We all have times when we feel alone and rejected. Carol's journey through pain and suffering and ultimately her growth in the Lord give us all hope to continue on through our journeys. This book encourages us to know that our true source of love, hope, and peace comes from our Heavenly Father. He will never leave or forsake us. He gives us His peace in the midst of our storms—He truly gives us beauty for ashes."

—Dr. Phyllis Arno, author, speaker, and co-founder of the
National Christian Counselors Association, ncca.org

"How do you deal with rejection, tragedy, and deception, then venture into uncharted waters and come out a far better person at the end? Carol walks us through the hurdles then reveals the secret to having a peace and joy that transcends all understanding. Bravo, Girl, for bearing your heart and soul so that someone else needn't travel that road alone."

—Don Honeywell, President, Face to
Faith Ministry, face2faith.org

"In *Enveloped*, Dr. Carol Erb draws from a deep well of personal heartache, experience, understanding, and insight. She shows all of us who have had our lives shattered and our hearts broken by disappointment and difficulties the way to find our path to a new normal and a hopeful future."

—Sandra Dopf Lee, co-author of the series
"The Next Steps after Divorce: Rebuilding Your
Life after Divorce," emergevictorious.com

"*Enveloped* is a true story of our friend whom we watched walk through many disappointments, obstacles, and insurmountable challenges. Carol had every 'right' to bury herself in self-pity and bitterness, but instead she pursued God's direction and will for her life. Her story inspires us to walk with a confident faith in our personal and sovereign God who 'will never leave us nor forsake us.'"

—Winston and Jayne Hodges, Marriage Mentoring Ministry,
capitalcommunitychurch.com

"Dr. Carol Erb has written a book from the heart that is sure to resonate with women who know the pain of their husbands' infidelity. If you're wondering what to do next in your journey of confusion, I recommend that you read *Enveloped*. You're sure to be blessed.

—Rob Jackson, licensed professional counselor,
writer, and national speaker, christiancounsel.com

ENVELOPED

FROM SHATTERED TO SECURE:
ONE WOMAN'S SEARCH FOR UNENDING LOVE

CAROL ERB, PH.D.

THOMAS NOBLE BOOKS

Thomas Noble Books
Wilmington, DE
www.thomasnoblebooks.com
ISBN: 978-0-9892357-9-2
Library of Congress Control Number: 2015907622
Printed in the United States of America
First Printing 2015
Cover design by 2FacedDesign.com
Editing by Gwen Hoffnagle

To my husband, Walt
"My beloved is mine and I am his."

—Song of Solomon 2:16

and

To my sons, Brent, Chad, and Jordan
"Behold, children are a gift from the Lord."

—Psalm 127:3

ACKNOWLEDGMENTS

· · · · · · ·

To my friends—When I was walking through the valley, I don't know how you stood listening to my sad story over and over again. You saw my raw emotion and gave me the space I needed to work through it all. Your friendship is treasured. I am a better person because of you. You will recognize yourselves in my story. You deserve medals of honor.

To my clients—You are so special to me. You are forever on my heart and mind. It has been such an honor to be God's helping hand to gently care for the tender places of your hearts and souls. You are the reason my journey has been so worthwhile. I understand you. Thank you for choosing me as your counselor and marriage coach. This book exists because you gave me the passion to write it.

To my church family—Over the last thirty-three years we studied God's Word, prayed, and fellowshipped together. Whether we studied and soaked in God's truth around a kitchen table, at the oceanside, or in a sanctuary, classroom, or restaurant, I am so blessed to have been in your company while mining the pearls of God's Word. May we continue to grow in grace and knowledge of Jesus Christ our Lord.

To my book coach, Lisa Canfield—You believed in me as a writer and assured me my story was worthy to be told. You held my hand and led the way. I am so happy I chose you to come alongside me as my book midwife. You were the very first person to read my manuscript. You became a friend on my journey. I loved working with you.

To my publisher, Lynne Klippel of the Thomas Noble Books family—God knew my publisher needed to be a woman. You have lovingly guided me down the publishing path. We have had many "ah-ha moments," "oohs," and "aahs," and undeniable direction from the Holy Spirit.

To my family-in-love—Thank you for sharing your dad with me. Your laughter and joy is contagious. I look forward to building even more family memories with you.

To my family—Mother, Bob, and Sims—God sovereignly chose you to accomplish His purposes in me. He has worked through you to develop character qualities in my life and to prepare me for my life's work and ministry. I thank God for you, love you more than you know, and pray we will forever be together in eternity.

To my beloved sons, Brent, Chad, and Jordan—When I was in the eighth grade I wanted to be a mother when I grew up, and I wanted three children. You have been God's reward and my greatest asset. I have learned more about the meaning of agape love through you than through any other source. I love you with a love that will never let you go. My highest prayer is that you have seen God in me and nothing matters more than living for Him.

To my daughter-in-law, Amanda—Before I knew you I prayed for you and purposed in my heart to love you. When I found out I was going to be a mother-in-law I read every book I could get my hands on because I wanted to be a good mother-in-law. Having a lovely daughter-in-law has made my role so enjoyable. You are the daughter I never had.

To my husband, Walt—From the moment we exchanged our first email you told me my words had an effect on you. You said over and over that I needed to tell my story. You have been the wind beneath my wings. You have fulfilled every promise you made me. You told me you would be my best friend, would love me to no end, and would do whatever it took to support me. You have shown me true love. God answered my prayer when I asked Him to look the world over for a husband. He chose you and I am everything I am because you love me. I love you with all my heart.

To my Lord—When I was searching for unending love You drew me by Your spirit and loved me first. I believed You... I put my full trust in You... I surrendered my life to You. I stand on tiptoe expectancy to see how You continue to fulfill Your perfect will in my life. "Now to Him who is able to do exceedingly abundantly beyond all that we ask or think, according to the power that works within us to Him be the glory..." (Ephesians 3:20–21).

To the others—Sometimes the greatest spiritual lessons come from those who weren't so loving. When you doubted me or were not interested in my dreams or my difficulties, you are the ones who kept me going as I pursued God's calling. I am grateful for you. My prayer is that you have found an unending love—His love. This book is for you, too.

CONTENTS

• • • • • • •

Letter to the Reader 15

1. Introduction 17
2. Child of Divorce 25
3. The Collapse 43
4. The End. 49
5. Picking up the Pieces.. 59
6. Back to School 67
7. The Dating Game. 79
8. Paradise 93
9. Home Again 113
10. Finally Home 127

Conclusion: Looking Forward. 137
Appendix: The Lord's Unending Love. 141
About the Author.. 143
Connect with Carol 145

Letter to the Reader

• • • • • • •

Dear Reader,

Chances are you are reading this book because you are hurting. You may be feeling alone and afraid of what your future holds. Whether the pain you are experiencing is due to a crumbling marriage, a loss, or a betrayal, you face confusion and struggle. Are you longing for another person who understands your gut-wrenching pain?

If so, then I have written this book for you.

In reading *Enveloped*, you might find yourself in its pages. You might recognize the same frightening emotions or crazy thoughts. You will find comfort in the pages of this book. You are not alone.

God is ever-present and promises that He will not leave you or forsake you no matter what difficulties arise in your life. He will watch over you and reveal His perfect will to you in a personal way. It may come to you through His written Word, answered prayer, something you read in this book, or the words of a stranger. You will know when you have received your answer when you feel the peace that only comes from God.

To help you apply some of the lessons of *Enveloped* to your journey, I've created a free downloadable workbook to use as you read it. I invite you to go to www.drcarolerb.com for your reader gift.

Whether you are on a personal search for unending love or coping with a challenge that causes pain, know that I think of you and pray for you as you seek your heart's desire.

With gladness and singleness of heart,
Carol

CHAPTER ONE

• • • • • • • •

INTRODUCTION

"Do not fear, for I am with you; Do not anxiously look about you, for I am your God. I will strengthen you, surely I will help you, Surely I will uphold you with My righteous right hand."

—Isaiah 41:10

THE IMAGE IS burned into my mind, never to be forgotten. My middle son, Chad, was cleaning his Dad's car. He came running into the house wanting to show me a matchbook he found in the car. Because this was no ordinary matchbook. It featured an image of voluptuous women, along with the name of a local topless bar. Chad asked me what was going on. I had no idea.

After he finished detailing the car, I told each of my three sons—who were ten, twelve, and fifteen at the time—that I needed to go run an errand, and that I would be home in a little while. I had an unstoppable compulsion to go to that topless bar.

Years later I came to believe that the Holy Spirit led me to that bar to uncover a hidden secret—a secret my husband had kept from me since the beginning of our marriage. But as I drove my husband's car into the parking lot of the Cue and Ale that afternoon, all I could think about was the connection between my husband and that matchbook, especially when I spotted a red Caravan that distinctly displayed the sign of the fish on the back window.

My car. Parked in that parking lot. My heart sank and horror swept over me. I walked into the bar and made my way through the crowd of people, scanning the room for my husband. Suddenly I felt an arm on my shoulder. I turned around and found myself staring into the eyes of a bouncer.

"Ma'am, this place is for members only."

His words hit me like a slap in the face. My husband was a member of this topless bar. Since I was not a member, the bouncer told me I would have to go sit by the door. Just then I spotted my husband. He was sitting at the bar—and a woman was rubbing his shoulders. I turned to the bouncer. "See that man with the yellow shirt on? Go get him!" And I dutifully headed to a seat by the door.

Up until that moment I had been so focused on finding my husband that I hadn't taken the time to look around. Now I did. The room was dimly lit, illuminated by swirling, colored lights. There was the stench of alcohol and the mustiness of cigarette smoke.

I turned my head to my left and I saw the stage. Before my eyes were topless dancers wearing nothing but G-strings, shimmying up and down poles. And in the center of the stage was a stand-alone Plexiglas shower with a dancer erotically performing as water streamed over her perfectly formed body.

It felt so evil being in there. What was a wife and mother who taught Bible studies at church doing in a topless bar at 5:30 in the afternoon? It all seemed so surreal. I was utterly helpless, sitting by myself in a chair in the corner, watching another woman caress my husband.

It was gut-wrenching.

The bouncer came back to my chair by the door. I pleaded with him to please go get that man in the yellow shirt. It felt like my eyes were shooting laser beams focused directly on my husband.

I waited some more. Then all of a sudden the lights came on and the music stopped. A voice came over the PA system announcing my husband's name: "Your wife is here and she is really upset!"

But my husband didn't move. Neither did the woman who was still rubbing his shoulders. They were oblivious. It was as though they were in their own world. Unbelievable.

I remained in my seat for what seemed like an eternity, and eventually the bouncer came back to my spot near the door. This time I made myself really clear. I *needed* him to go get my husband. He did.

Finally my husband got up and walked through the crowd to where I stood waiting by the door. He walked right up to me and took my hand. I looked to see if he was wearing his wedding band. I didn't know what to expect, but he had it on. He said, "I guess we need to go home."

I replied that I was not going home, but I would meet him at his office.

As I left the bar, the shock hit me full swing. It felt like I had lead in my shoes. I methodically walked to the car and turned the engine on. I felt like a robot. Slowly I drove to my husband's office. At least I had enough clarity to stop at a convenience store on the way to get a Coca-Cola to settle my stomach.

When I arrived at the office, he was waiting for me. The first words out of his mouth were, "I was afraid you were going to punch me out."

I looked at him and said, "I'm not like that." Then I asked him what he was doing in a topless bar.

His response? "I can go to these places and be just whoever I want to be."

At that moment I suddenly envisioned him dressed in a Superman costume. I have a dry, wry sense of humor that I tend to use as a coping mechanism. And it did provide a brief moment of comic relief. Sadly, it was only a moment.

My husband denied anything was "going on" beyond the revelation that he frequented topless bars. That alone was more than I could bear. But it was just the beginning of discovering who I'd married.

Our sons competed in racquetball tournaments, and on Wednesday nights they would play with their dad at the local sports center where they trained. One evening after teaching Bible study, I decided I would drop by to watch their matches. I could hear the familiar cracking sound of balls hitting the court walls as I walked downstairs, and began peering through the various view windows to spot which courts my boys were playing on. I noticed the weight-training room door was open and happened to glance inside.

I had to take a second glance. My husband was in there, standing beside a workout machine, helping a woman with her workout. One of my sons was also there and came over to greet me. I asked him who Dad was with. He explained that she was one of Dad's college friends, and that they had met her the previous fall when they had traveled to a racquetball tournament in the eastern part of the state.

I had met my husband in college. That woman was no friend of his or ours. In fact she looked just like the woman who had been rubbing his back in the topless bar.

I thought to myself that my husband was a liar. I immediately decided I would introduce myself to this woman. I walked straight into the workout room, and my husband's face turned white as a sheet. I stated my name and told the woman who I was. My husband told me the woman's name. She sheepishly shook my hand and looked down. My husband said he guessed it was time to go home. This time I agreed.

My sons packed their sports bags and the five of us walked out together. Brent and Jordan headed toward their dad's car. Chad chose to ride with me.

Except I did not go home. I turned the car around and went back to the racquetball facility to look for the woman I had seen with my husband. She was still right where I had left her. She couldn't have been a day older than twenty-two.

I asked her if I could talk to her for a minute, and then asked her if she was in love with my husband. She replied that she liked him a lot. I asked her where she worked. She said she worked at the Cue and Ale. I asked her how she had met my husband. She said he usually came in on Friday afternoons. I looked at her as though I could bore a hole through her and said, "My marriage is very precious to me." There was an obvious tension between us. I paused and walked away.

When I arrived home, my husband asked me what had taken me so long. I told him I had gone back to the sports center to talk to the woman he had been working out with. He had a look of fear in his eyes. He explained that he had met her at a real estate luncheon. I told him I knew he was lying. I knew that she worked as a dancer at the Cue and Ale.

Now I had a lot of questions that needed answers. He went silent. I hit another stone wall.

My home phone rang. It was a friend of mine who attended our church. Her daughter had gotten married that day, and since my husband was the chairman of building and grounds at the church, he had gone to meet her there so she could return the chairs she had borrowed for the wedding. Except my friend was running late. And she'd been calling the church hoping to let my husband know that she'd be late returning the chairs, but she just kept getting a busy signal. Would I mind giving my husband the message?

I told her not to worry. I would go to the church and deliver the message to my husband in person. Because I had another motive.

Upon my arrival, I quietly opened the unlocked door and tip-toed down the hall. I knew that church like the back of my hand, so it was easy to find an empty office to duck into. I carefully picked up the telephone receiver. I heard my husband's voice on the phone.

He was talking to a woman. He said her name. It was the woman from the Cue and Ale. He was planning his next tryst with her for the following day. He told her he would tell me he was going to play golf. I hung the phone up with a raging storm brewing inside. I walked around the corner to the office where my husband was talking and waited outside the door for him to finish his conversation. He walked out and spotted me and stopped like a deer in headlights. I just stood there and glared at him.

Then I told him I knew what was going on. I told him he was in big trouble. He said I was right.

I thought back over the first year we were married. There had been signs; I was just too naïve to be able to sort them out. One evening my husband seemed really restless. He left our den and returned with a change of clothes. He said, "I think I am going to shoot some pool." It was 10:00 in the evening and I was ready for bed. He had never wanted to go out and play pool before. I asked him not to go, but he assured me he would be gone no longer than an hour.

After midnight I started to get scared. I called the only friend I knew who wouldn't mind a late-night phone call. She came over to our house and we went out in the car to look for him. It was pouring down rain—a stormy night. But not nearly as stormy as what I was feeling on the inside. A woman has an intuition when something isn't right. And this wasn't right.

We drove all over town, but we couldn't find my husband. I told her to go back home and I would just wait by myself.

How long do you wait before you start calling hospitals or the police department? I sat at our living room window and watched for headlights coming down our street. Finally, at 1:00 in the morning, he drove up the driveway. I was relieved and angry wrapped up in one big ball of emotion.

When he walked in the door I burst into tears. He asked me what was wrong. I told him that he had promised me he would only be gone an hour. I told him that I had been worried that something bad had happened to him. He said he had lost track of time, and that he was sorry.

I had no idea that this wouldn't be the last time. It was only the beginning.

CHAPTER TWO

· · · · · · ·

CHILD OF DIVORCE

"Before I formed you in the womb I knew you, And before you were born I consecrated you; I have appointed you a prophet to the nations."

—*Jeremiah 1:5*

I WAS BORN in Lumberton, North Carolina, a southeastern town located halfway between New York and Florida. I'm the older of two children—my brother, Sims, is three-and-a-half years younger than I. And Sims and I were about as opposite as they come. I had dark hair and he was a towheaded blond. I was the babbling brook and he was the dry sea. I was the talker and he was the listener. We really got along as children. I barely remember us ever having a disagreement.

My parents, on the other hand, were like oil and water. To say that opposites attract is an understatement where they were concerned. My father, Fletcher, was a pharmacist. He owned his own drugstore called Dean's Pharmacy—the kind of pharmacy where he knew his customers on a first-name basis. As a child, I loved to go there after school. My friends did, too. An invitation to go home with me meant a trip to the drugstore where we would read Archie comic books, drink Coca-Colas, eat BBQ potato chips, and split a bag of M&Ms.

I loved my daddy. He was playful and kind of goofy. He used to give me what he called the "zizz," otherwise known as a "noogie." He would ball up his fist and rub his knuckles back and forth on my head making a "zizzing" sound. He played the Hambone song, clapping his hands and slapping his legs singing, "Hambone walks, Hambone talks… Hambone doggone!" I wondered if he had made it up, but years later I found out it was a real song when I found videos of the Hambone song on YouTube. My daddy was a kid at heart. He was the tender-hearted type.

My mother, Hope, was the opposite of my daddy. She was a French and English teacher, and a private, serious sort of person. I learned proper English by osmosis, along with the good manners she laid out as guidelines to live by. Dinnertime at our table was like being in a classroom. I heard, "Put your hands in your lap," "Move your elbows off the table," and "Eat with your mouth closed" more times than I could count. If I got my verb tenses mixed up I was immediately corrected.

Needless to say, English was a course in school that I had no problem with. I heard it correctly at home. And I also placed out of two years of French in college.

Mother was very cultured. She took me to community concerts and exposed me to the finer things in life. She made sure that I took piano and ballet lessons. But it was hard to connect and get close to Mother. When I asked her questions she would often say "I don't know" or "I don't remember" if it was a topic she didn't want to talk about. When I started my period in the seventh grade, I was so scared to talk to her about it that I wrote her a note.

I don't remember ever hearing my parents say "I love you" to each other. They were not at all demonstrative—I never saw them hug or kiss or hold hands. Looking back, the only time I really remember their seeming happy was when they were preparing to go to a Cotillion Club dance. Mother had a store-bought teased-up hairdo and was wearing sparkly earrings and a matching brace-let. Her shoes were dyed to match her flowing blue gown. Daddy was sporting a tuxedo with a fancy blue ruffled shirt that matched Mother's dress. His shoes were shiny patent leather, and his cologne smelled good. They were smiling and their spirits were light on that night. I had never seen them look or act that way before, nor have I since.

Mostly they were the opposite. Sometimes I would hear them arguing at night behind their bedroom door. My stomach would twist into knots as I listened to their raised voices. I would lie in bed until I couldn't take it any longer, and then, with every ounce of courage I could muster, I would go to their door, knock on it, and beg them to stop. I remember feeling envious that my brother could sleep through it all.

At an early age I had the ability to detect when others were in emotional distress. I was sensitive to people who hurt on the inside. Many of my childhood friends were those who came from broken homes or seemed to have hidden pain. I was able to sense when they needed a listening ear, and because of this they would seek me out to talk to about their problems.

But when it came to my parents I felt helpless. I was powerless to change the situation.

I felt terribly alone.

The Warning

After high school graduation I attended East Carolina University in Greenville and pursued a degree in recreation therapy. My university did not offer a professional counseling program, and I chose recreation therapy because it seemed to be a discipline in which I could use my gifts and talents.

I went home for Christmas break during my freshman year. We were sitting in our living room opening Christmas presents when Daddy left the room to get something to drink. At that moment Mother said the strangest thing to me and my brother. Out of nowhere she said, "This may be our last Christmas together."

I couldn't wrap my mind around that statement. I knew she did not like the fanfare of holidays and decorating—all that Christmas cheer was burdensome to her. In fact, my brother and I usually decorated the tree ourselves. Still, I thought that not having Christmas together anymore as a family was a crazy thing to say. But it turned out she meant it.

THE DEPARTURE

During my summer break from college I worked as a lifeguard at our country club—the first female lifeguard in my hometown. I would arrive by 9:30 AM and work all day until my shift ended at 5:30 PM.

It was a sunny day in June. I was just a month short of celebrating my nineteenth birthday. My mother dropped me off at work, as she often did. As I stepped out of the car she said, "I'm leaving and I'm taking your brother with me. I left a hundred dollars under your pillow." And, "Don't tell your father."

What? I felt like I had just been hit by an airbag; her words knocked the wind out of me. I had no time to react. I just stood there watching her blue Chevrolet Caprice disappear down the road, keeping my eyes on the car until I could no longer see the taillights.

I felt numb. All that day I was in a kind of fog. I had trouble concentrating. But of course I didn't tell my fellow lifeguards what had just happened. I wasn't even exactly sure what had just happened. It's a good thing no one needed me to rescue them that day or they might have drowned.

Later that afternoon I noticed that I had started to break out in a rash that looked like spots. Even worse, one of the other lifeguards noticed, too! He said, "Carol, you look like you have the "ick."

I asked, "What is that?"

He told me that the ick was a deadly disease that caused white spots on aquarium fish. It attacked their gills, and their scales deteriorated, and if they weren't treated they would die.

That made me laugh. But inside I was crying. As the time drew closer to go home it dawned on me: *"Who is going to tell Daddy that Mother left?"*

I realized it was going to be me.

BREAKING THE NEWS

I arrived home promptly at 6:00 PM, showered, and dressed. I had called my boyfriend to tell him what had happened, and he came over to comfort me, but he left before Daddy was due to arrive home from work.

I was alone—and full of dread.

Daddy arrived around 7:00 PM. Immediately he came into my bedroom and asked the fateful question, "Where is your mother?"

My heart was beating out of my chest by now, and those terrible words came out of my mouth. "She left."

"What do you mean she left?"

I told him what had happened that morning; that when she had dropped me off at work she had said she was leaving and told me not to tell him.

"Why didn't you call me? I could have tried to stop her." Then Daddy paused. "Where is Sims?"

I told him that she had taken Sims with her. We were both in so much pain at this point that we didn't know where to turn. We hugged each other and Daddy started to cry. He sat down on the small green loveseat in my bedroom. I sat at the foot of my bed. I wanted to comfort him, but at the same time I needed comfort, too. I didn't know what to do. I was grasping at straws.

I spotted a small book that a college friend had given me sitting on my nightstand—*The Prophet*, by Kahlil Gibran. I flipped to the table of contents and turned to a chapter entitled "On Pain." Thinking the book might be able to help, I read the following aloud:

Your pain is the breaking of the shell that encloses your understanding. Even as the stone of the fruit must break, that its heart may stand in the sun, so must you know pain.

That book offered no comfort. At that moment it was meaningless. I looked at Daddy and felt totally helpless. I had nothing more to offer him. Zippy-poo.

That night was a sleepless one. I tossed and turned as the realization sunk in that something terrible had just happened to our family. We would never be the same again. I didn't know how to deal with my heartache. I certainly did not consider talking with a professional who might have been able to help. I had no idea how people did that, so I kept my pain inside.

At least things got back to semi-normal a few weeks later when Sims came back home. He had finally been able to call home, and obtained money for a bus ticket back—from the state of Virginia. Mother had moved into an apartment there. That's when we learned that they weren't alone in that apartment. Mother had left Daddy for another man. Which, I suppose, sort of explained things.

That fall I returned to college to begin my sophomore year. My boyfriend had been the one stable person in my life since we had met during my senior year in high school when I was the head cheerleader and he was on the football team. He was my first love, and since we went to the same college, we continued to date in college. But that winter he started doing drugs.

I was not into that scene. It scared me, and I wanted no part of it. I thought that eventually my boyfriend would come to his senses and choose me over the drugs. But he didn't. So we broke up. I had lost my mother to another man, my boyfriend to drugs, and now my father was slipping into depression.

I had never felt so alone.

THE PROMISE

After my sophomore year of college I returned home for the summer again. But the word *home* was stretching it—it was nothing like the home I had left behind when I had gone back to school after Easter break. It had been totally cleaned out. Furniture was missing. The hardwood floors were barren. The Oriental rugs were gone. The artwork on the walls had been removed. Even the refrigerator, washing machine, and dryer were missing. It looked like burglars had broken in and taken almost everything we had.

But we hadn't been robbed. I learned that's what happens in a divorce settlement.

Determined to make our house into a home again, I assumed the role of mother. Instead of spending the summer on vacation, or at the beach, when I wasn't working at the pool I spent it at the laundromat, doing the family's wash. I met some interesting people washing clothes that summer, but overall it was a very humbling experience. When I wasn't chatting with the other laundry-doers, I used the time to read and to write letters to my sorority sisters from college, who were no doubt having much more fun that summer than I was.

With Daddy's help we slowly began to turn our house into a home again. He had always been a good provider, and we didn't have much trouble replacing the stuff that my mother had acquired. But Daddy was having a hard time getting past his grief. When I would come home at night after being out with friends and go to Daddy's bedroom door to let him know I was home and to say goodnight, the door would be locked. I would stand there and knock on his door until he opened it. I couldn't go to sleep until I had said goodnight because I needed to know that he was okay. And I had reason to worry. Sometimes he would be so groggy after I came home that I think he must have been self-medicating with prescription drugs to deal with his pain. I started to panic deep down inside, worried that one night I would knock and knock at the door and he wouldn't open it because he was dead from an overdose.

That summer I made a promise to myself: I would never, ever get divorced. Divorce hurts people.

ROB

In the spring of my sophomore year I decided I wanted to try out for my college cheerleading squad. Tryouts wouldn't be until the fall of the next year, but there were practices where we could learn the dance routines and the stunts so we could perfect them ahead of time. One of my sorority sisters knew a guy named Rob who was already on the cheerleading squad and was helping out at the practices. I decided to go find this Rob, and joined his group to work on my technique.

Wanda was my best friend from high school, and that summer Wanda and I drove to Fayetteville, about thirty minutes north of Lumberton, to go dancing. I loved to dance. We went to a really nice bar called the Skyline that was on top of the Wachovia Bank building overlooking the city. It was so much nicer than college bars, with glass stretching from the ceiling to the floor and the city lights all sparkly at night.

Wanda and I met up with some of her friends when I suddenly spotted Rob. We caught each other's eye. I said, "I think I know you. I'm trying out for cheerleading at East Carolina and you helped me with some of the stunts." I told him I was from Lumberton. I learned he was from Fayetteville.

Then he asked me the magic question. "Would you like to dance?"

Of course I said yes. He was a great dancer. And not only that, he was a gentleman. He asked me to sit at his table, pulled my chair out for me, and ordered me a drink. We danced and talked all night, and he was a great conversationalist, too. But eventually it was time for me to go.

Wanda and I went back to the Skyline the following Saturday night and Rob was there again. He found me and we danced and talked all night, and this time he even walked me down to the car when the evening was over. I summoned up the courage to invite him to a party in Lumberton the following weekend. He said he would try to come, and I hoped against all hope that he would. But he never showed.

The next Friday I had come home from lifeguarding and had just showered and begun to dress, when I looked out my bedroom window and saw a car parked out front. A young guy was walking up the walk. I did a double-take. It was Rob!

I quickly filled my brother Sims in on who this Rob was before he had the chance to ring the doorbell. Sims answered the door, showed Rob to the den, and told him to wait for me there while I finished getting dressed. While Sims was getting Rob settled, I told Daddy about Rob as well. Sims left to go out with friends, and Daddy left, too, introducing himself to Rob as he walked out. I finished dressing and went into the den.

Rob explained that he was visiting his roommate at the lake, which was south of Lumberton, and thought he would surprise me on the way home to Fayetteville. I was shocked. And so happy! He took me out for pizza. We were never at a loss for words.

Rob told me later that he had been worried I was getting ready for a date since my brother and father seemed to be expecting someone, and that obviously, since he came to surprise me, he wasn't the date. I told him that I had spotted him out the window and filled in my brother and father about who he was before he had rung the doorbell. We laughed. He had been worried that he would be the one to answer the doorbell when my date arrived!

But as much as we seemed to hit it off, that was the last I saw of Rob. At least for a while.

Later that summer I returned to college for my junior year and moved into the Alpha Phi sorority house. One day I was walking on campus and saw one of the cheerleaders. I told her to tell Rob hello for me. I received a message from him the next day. He left his phone number, asking me to return his call. I did, and we soon began dating exclusively.

In October Rob told me that he loved me. I was falling in love, too.

THE RED FLAG

I tried out for cheerleading as planned, with Rob as my partner. We had perfected the stunts and had even created a new one that no one had ever attempted. My routine was flawless. But I didn't make it. I was crushed.

A few months later Rob found out that the head cheerleader had voted to blackball me through secret ballot. He said she was jealous of me. Rob was so chivalrous that he actually quit cheer-leading because of that. We continued to date and grew closer. Not making the squad didn't turn out to be so bad; I had found an amazing boyfriend.

Except for one little thing: No matter how often I asked, he absolutely flat-out refused to talk about his previous relationships with girls. Maybe it was a red flag, but at the time I decided that he just valued his privacy. It wasn't a deal-breaker; not when everything else was so perfect.

Our relationship continued to progress. I met his family for the first time at the homecoming game. They were so different from my family—he had four siblings and his parents seemed so close! It was a little intimidating, but I loved being around them. It was the kind of family I wished I had.

LOVE, MARRIAGE, AND GOD

Rob graduated from college at the end of my junior year and went to work as an appraiser at his father's real estate company. I graduated a year later and moved to Fayetteville, where I began working as a recreation therapist at a psychiatric hospital and, of course, waited for Rob to take our relationship to the next level.

And waited… and waited…. Okay, so I had to press the issue a little bit. However, on October 13th, 1978, it finally happened. Rob proposed to me. And of course I accepted.

One day after Rob and I had announced our engagement, we were sitting around the family table at his parents' home. I was seated beside my future father-in-law, who was at the head of the table. Rob's dad looked me dead in the eye and said, "There will be no divorce in our family." I could have taken issue with that statement, but I didn't. After seeing what my parents had gone through, divorce was simply not an option for me. I was getting ready to marry into a family in which marriage was placed in high regard. It made me feel secure.

We scheduled the required premarital counseling sessions with my pastor. At our initial session he asked for each of our histories and said, "Well, because you were raised in the same church denomination, we don't have any problems here." That was the extent of our premarital counseling. According to my pastor, we were good to go.

We married on March 24th, 1979. Finally I had found that love I had been searching for. I was sure that being a wife and a mother would provide me with all the love and stability I had been longing for.

I would never feel alone again.

THE GIFT TABLE

We spent a blissful honeymoon in Florida. I felt so proud and happy to be Rob's wife. On our way home we stopped in Lumberton to pack up all the wedding gifts that had been on display in the dining room of Daddy's home. But Daddy had other plans for those gifts. As we prepared to box everything up, he asked us if we could please leave them behind for one more week.

Daddy had loved all the festivities surrounding our wedding and was planning one last party at the house that weekend. He wanted to show off my gifts to his guests. They did look spectacular. The gift tables lined the dining room. The tables were beautiful with flowing white linens overlaid with yellow netting. White bows hung to the floor, and a crystal chandelier glittered above the table. But those gifts weren't just pretty decorations; they were things Rob and I needed to start our life together!

I tried to explain. "Daddy, these are our sheets and towels. We need our china to eat on and our pots and pans to cook with. We can't leave them another week."

He pleaded with me. Finally I had an idea. "We have a polaroid camera in the car. Why don't we take photos and you can show your friends the gifts that way?" It sounded like the perfect solution to me. Daddy wasn't entirely satisfied, but he complied.

HOME AND FAMILY

Rob and I lived on the same street that his parents lived on. I realize that might sound like a nightmare to a lot of people, but I loved being near his family. Both his parents treated me as though I were their daughter by choice. And I automatically gained two sisters-in-law and two brothers-in-law. I felt so blessed to have family around.

One of the biggest and happiest changes came at Christmastime. There was an Advent wreath displayed in the living room at Rob's parents' home, and I had no idea what it was for. Someone explained that each Sunday prior to Christmas one of the family members would read a scripture and light a candle.

One Sunday I was asked to do a reading. I felt so warm and accepted and loved being a part of my new family. Unlike my mother, who never cared much for Christmas, my mother-in-law loved the season. She went all out—decorating, baking, and inviting friends over on Christmas Eve for Christmas goodies and punch. I loved her beautiful silver punch bowl and ladle, and the way she set the table with her Lenox Christmas china. It was wonderful—a joyous holiday celebration.

But I didn't care just about the festive part of the season—I started getting more interested in the reason *for* the season. I was starting to become more interested in my spirituality and my relationship with God. I began attending church more regularly than I had, and decided that I really wanted my own Bible. And that Christmas my in-laws surprised me with my first Bible. My name was engraved on it, and I'll never forget how beautiful it was and how proud I was of it.

I was working at Cumberland County Mental Health when one of my co-workers invited me to a dinner meeting called Christian Women's Club, which was held at a local country club. I loved the experience and kept going to the meetings. They were like girls' night out for me. They always featured an inspirational speaker, music, and some special thing that was of interest to women, like a fashion show. Of course part of the fun was getting dressed up and going out and being with other women. But there was more to it than that. I noticed that there was something different about the women who put on those meetings. I couldn't put my finger on it, but they all seemed to have so much joy. I wondered where it came from. And I wanted to experience it, too.

Rob and I continued to go to church, but I hungered for something more. In my mind I kept thinking that there had to be more to God than what I was experiencing at the time. I was doing all these things to get close to God, but it wasn't enough. Something was missing.

One evening I was sitting in the den with Rob and had a troubling thought. I asked my husband, "Rob, if I were to die, do you think I would go to heaven?"

He said, "Oh, I'm sure you will."

I put my full trust in Rob, but his answer just did not satisfy me. I needed more than my husband's opinion. I wanted to know what God said about how to go to heaven, and my husband couldn't give me that answer.

At that month's Christian Women's Club dinner meeting a woman stood behind a podium to speak, and the things she said really made me think. I felt a connection with her. Her words helped me understand what was missing inside of me. I had this hidden fear inside of me. Sometimes I worried that I was insignificant and not valued. Occasionally this caused me turmoil. At that moment I realized what I needed. I wanted to know that God loved me. I wanted someone in my life who would forgive me for my mistakes, understand me at a deep level, and love me with a love that would never let me go—an unending love.

THE PRAYER

Life went on exactly as it should. And two years after we married, our first child, Brent, was born. Now we really were a family.

It was September 17th, 1982. I thought it was going to be just another day. I began my duties as a young mother. Little did I know that God was waiting for me.

I went to my bedside. I understood that I could invite Jesus into my heart, but I still had no idea how to pray. *How do I talk to God?* I said the simplest, most heartfelt prayer I knew: *"God, I am Yours. I am giving You my life to do whatever You wish."*

On that day I trusted Jesus Christ to be my Savior and Lord. I knew that was the most important decision I would ever make in my life, and that from that day forward I would never be the same.

The first person I told about my decision was Rob's sister. Next was my friend and co-worker. They were both happy for me. But I was scared to tell Rob. It would crush me if he brushed off my decision as if it were no big deal. Or worse, if he belittled me and rejected me.

Despite my fears I decided I would make telling him into a celebration. I asked my mother-in-law to watch Brent. I ordered fresh flowers from the florist. I set the table with our finest china and silver. I prepared Rob's favorite meal. And after dinner I told Rob I had something important to tell him. I mustered all the courage I had and explained to him that I had invited Jesus into my heart. He asked me to sit on his lap. I put my head on his shoulder and he held me there. He told me that he was proud of me. Relief poured over me as Rob seemed to share my joy. All was well in my world.

MOTHER AND BOB

While I was building a life with Rob, Mother and her significant other, Bob, had been building their own life together. They eventually moved from Virginia to Chapel Hill, North Carolina, where they built an addition onto my grandmother's home and began living with her.

This brought my mother closer to me. So I went to visit her and was introduced to Bob for the first time. He was outgoing, friendly, and conversational. The three of us headed off to the mall to window-shop. I observed my mother walking hand-in-hand with Bob. She was laughing and smiling, with an infectious smile and a girlish giggle. I had never seen her like that in the entire nineteen years she had been married to Daddy.

Mother and Bob stopped by a jewelry store and looked into the display window, peering at diamonds and whispering to each other. My mother was like a giddy teenager. A few months later Rob and I attended their wedding, which was held in my grandmother's home. My brother attended, as did Bob's son. Life was going on.

FORGIVENESS

Over the years of my marriage I continued attending Bible study and growing in my relationship with God. I learned about forgiveness. God knows what He is doing when He says we must forgive. There are no shortcuts. It has to be done His way.

I had had a lot of pain inside when my mother left our home. I needed to clean out the resentments I held against her. I didn't want to hurt anymore and I wanted to work on improving my relationship with my mother. But forgiveness is hard work. It takes a lot of faith.

And then one day during one of her visits, I opened my heart. I told Mother how much it had hurt me when she left. And I forgave her for the way she exited our lives. She didn't say anything, but tears ran down her face. She had hidden pain inside, too. We hugged each other and I felt an overwhelming love for my mother surround me. Forgiveness was accomplished and the healing of our relationship could begin. It was a tender moment. Unfortunately my family would not be whole or healed for long.

THE PHONE CALL

It was a cold day in February. I had just come home from taking my sons to their respective schools and had settled down with a steaming hot cup of coffee to read my daily devotional. The phone rang. It was my brother. It was the type of call that you dread.

"Something terrible has happened to Daddy."

I asked what had happened.

"He killed himself."

"How?" I asked.

"He shot himself. You've got to get here quick." Sims hung up.

One thing I have learned about myself: When there is an emergency, I become inordinately calm. I picked up the phone and methodically called Rob, my pastor, and a dear friend. I then headed to the bathroom and started putting on my makeup. It was like I was moving in slow motion.

As I looked at myself in the mirror, scriptures flooded my soul:

"Do not boast about tomorrow, for you do not know what a day may bring forth."

"I will not leave you, nor forsake you, for I love you with an everlasting love."

At that moment the Holy Spirit was at work as my Comforter.

The drive to Lumberton took thirty minutes, but it felt like thirty days. When Rob and I arrived we immediately went to the drugstore. It was now a crime scene. Yellow caution tape surrounded the store where I had been so proud and happy to take my friends after school. I was told that one of Daddy's employees had found his lifeless body draped on the white vinyl sofa where customers would wait while their prescriptions were being filled. She had found him there when she went to open the store that morning.

We went to Daddy's house after that. On the coffee table in the den lay his personal effects. His college class ring, wedding band, and photos of my brother Sims and me, our spouses, and his grandchildren. In the bedroom on his bed lay a suicide note, with detailed instructions and cash for our immediate needs. In the note Daddy laid out his end-of-life wishes. It was his last act of love toward Sims and me.

In his Bible there were more handwritten notes to me and my brother, as well as to his pastor and his brothers and sisters. He had underlined selected scriptures and written "I believe" beside each passage. The note to me specifically stated that he hoped I would forgive him for ending his life this way, but to continue on in the precious name of Jesus—and that he would see me in heaven one day.

The weekend before Daddy took his life, he came to my home for a visit. We were sitting in the living room and he asked me for prayer. He didn't tell me what he needed prayer for, but I prayed for him nonetheless. After he left that weekend I thought maybe he was planning to propose to a lady he had been dating for some time. I had no idea he was planning his death.

I knew that Daddy had struggled with depression. I wish he would have reached out for professional help. Talking to someone might have saved his life.

After that horrible day I could have wrestled with "I could have, I should have, I ought to have"… better known as blame, shame, and guilt. I could have agonized endlessly over "Why didn't I see it?" But instead I chose to rest in God's sovereignty.

Even so, my pain was agonizing, intense, overpowering. One night I woke myself up with tears streaming down my face. I was grieving the loss of my Daddy even while I was sleeping. I was disturbed by the brutal way in which Daddy had died. I could not get the gunshot wound to the head out of my mind. I was so overcome by grief that I became concerned that I might need medical attention.

I asked Rob to pray for me. I lay quietly beside him on the couch as he began prayer. The Lord Christ showed up in a powerful way. During prayer, a distinct thought came to my mind: *"Look upon Me, they stuck a spear in My Side."* Instantly I was able to replace Daddy's wound by superimposing upon it the piercing of Christ. I began to sing praise songs aloud, which then turned to dancing before the Lord. Even in what was my darkest moment, He delivered me. But there would be more dark moments to come.

CHAPTER THREE

• • • • • • •

THE COLLAPSE

"For it is written, 'He will command his
angels concerning you, to guard you.'"

—*Luke 4:10*

I LIKE TO watch the reruns of a TV drama series called *Lie to Me*. The main character in the show is a detection expert named Cal Lightman. He can read body language, emotions, and facial microexpressions to detect whether or not someone is lying.

This probably fascinates me because when it came to my marriage I was certainly no detection expert! But it's not that I never had any suspicions. Marriage to Rob came with a boatload of contradictions. He was occasionally late coming home, and when he was late he would walk in armed with the most elaborate excuses, like he ran out of gas and had to walk a mile to find someone at home to get a ride to the gas station. Or his phone hadn't rung when I called. Or there must have been something wrong with the phone because he had been in the car when I called.

I am extremely sensitive to cigarette smoke, which shouldn't have been an issue because according to Rob he was not a smoker. But sometimes he would come home and his clothes, his hands, and his breath would all smell like cigarette smoke. How could he smell like smoke if he wasn't smoking? Still he would deny it. He was trapped in a car with clients who smoked. Or he had stopped by an office where the employees were smoking. So why did I keep finding cigarettes under the car seat or in the glove compartment? I remember looking at him and saying, "If you can lie to me about your smoking, it scares me to think of what else you could lie to me about."

Once I was looking over one of our savings account statements and noticed a $500 withdrawal. I never withdrew money from the account. I confronted Rob about it and he immediately said, "It must be a bank error. I'll straighten it out." He didn't.

Every year before we began planning our family vacation at the beach, I would beg him to promise me he would not go out at night and leave me alone with the boys. He would promise. But like clockwork, once our vacation was in full swing and there was no turning back, Rob would say he was just going to fish off the pier that was in view of our condo. "I'll be back in an hour. I just want to see if the fish are biting."

And then he would disappear. He wouldn't return until the middle of the night. From our upstairs bedroom I could see the bridge that stretched from the mainland across the water to Ocean Isle Beach, North Carolina. I would try to stay calm by counting car headlights coming over the bridge, trying to decide whether the headlights belonged to our Dodge Caravan. As the hours ticked by I would become almost panic-stricken, feeling trapped and helpless as a young mother with a baby, a preschooler, and an elementary-school-aged son. What if something had happened to Rob? When do you call the sheriff or the nearest emergency room?

Of course he would eventually come home. And the cycle would begin again. I would cry tears of relief, and then become angry. Then all Rob's excuses would start pouring forth. The fish weren't biting at the pier nearby, so he had to drive farther south.

Not once did he bring a fish home. And he never smelled like fish. But something was definitely fishy.

I started to feel like I was not important enough to be told the truth. And I hated feeling that way—it was emotionally exhausting. Being in a marriage with somebody who lies is difficult. I cared about Rob. I loved him. But his constant lying was causing a disconnect between us.

I talked to close friends about what was happening in my marriage, hoping to minimize my distress and maybe even find some answers. Of course they were happy to provide me with emotional support, but my fear was in not knowing where the lying was headed, and that no matter how hard I tried with Rob, I couldn't make it stop.

Still, it just didn't seem serious enough to talk to someone about on a professional level. And today I know that I was not alone in believing that. Research shows that couples don't get help until it is six years too late. By the six-year mark a couple has usually started their family and is putting the children first rather than the marriage. They are no longer giving one another their undivided attention. Busyness and independent behaviors start creeping into the marriage and become the biggest obstacles for maintaining the feeling of romantic love.

Despite the hard times, Rob had a good side. He was welcoming and loved having friends and family over. Our home always had an open door. He was a great conversationalist and was very generous to others. Rob was also a good dad. Before little league softball or basketball season began, mothers would call our house because they wanted to find out what day Rob's team practiced so they could make sure their son signed up for his team.

Rob would help me set up for Ladies' Bible Studies, and would type my weekly newsletter. We were in a couples Bible study group and Sunday school class together, and enjoyed the company of our Christian friends.

One year for my birthday he surprised me by inviting my inner circle of friends to my favorite restaurant. He left a single red rose at each lady's place setting. A beautiful bouquet of roses numbering each year since I had been born graced the table.

At the surprise party I threw for Rob for his fortieth birthday, his mother called him a "prince of a son" in front of all our guests. And he seemed to be. He was caring, even-tempered, and thoughtful.

On the outside we looked like the perfect couple. But as you already know, I was about to learn that we were anything but perfect.

THE LAST WEEKEND

The days following my discovery of Rob's affair passed by in a blur. But some aspects of our life as a family remained the same. So I accompanied Rob and our three sons to Charlotte, North Carolina, for a racquetball tournament that was being held at a YMCA—something I often did on the weekends so the boys could compete in tournaments. I didn't know it then, but I was raising future world, national, and state racquetball champions. What I did know, or at least suspect, was that this might be our last weekend together as a family. I was heavy-hearted.

When we arrived at the Y, we got the boys checked in at the front desk, looked over the draw sheets, and prepared to watch their first match. And then it happened. No doubt the emotional stress I was feeling triggered it. It starts the same way every time. I see dots, spots, and zigzag lines all floating across my field of vision. My hand and face start to tingle and go numb. And then, the pain—this vice-like, gripping, tightening pain in my head. It was excruciating. I was getting a full-blown migraine. I needed to find a place to lie down.

This was a top-notch YMCA, and it had a wellness center, but it was closed for the weekend. Thankfully a staff member had a key and opened the door to the center. It was tranquil and peaceful in there. He helped me up on the examining table, packed my head in ice, and covered me with a blanket. Rob made sure I was settled and the boys came in to check on me, but by now the matches were in full swing and I was left by myself.

Alone.

THE VISITOR

I lay still as I tried to deal with the pain. But the physical pain did not compare to the emotional and spiritual pain I was feeling. Although the room was quiet, there was nothing quiet about the thoughts that were swirling around in my mind.

I looked over my shoulder to my left and saw an African-American man standing against the wall. He spoke softly, saying, "I heard you were not feeling well." I told him I was getting a migraine and that the staff had brought me here. Then tears began streaming down my face. I began pouring my heart out to this strange man. I told him the story of everything that was happening in my life, from the matchbook my son had found to the topless bar to the revelation that my husband was having an affair. I shared my fear that this was the last weekend we would spend together as a family. Hearing those words spoken aloud was just… crushing.

The man asked me if I would like for him to stay with me for a while. I said yes. Then I looked closer. The man had gentleness about him. Something was different. At that moment I couldn't help wondering out loud, "You're an angel, aren't you?"

His answer? "Just call me James."

I believe with all my heart that God had sent James to me at that moment. I told James how I had given my life to Christ, and what had happened since. We shared scriptures together. James reminded me of stories in the Bible of how great men and women of God had overcome various trials and temptations. God used them in a mighty way.

James sang to me. He prayed for me. He stayed by my side for three solid hours. He kept saying to me, "Just trust Him." That message held me through all the pain. God was going to get me through this.

As lunchtime approached, my migraine had miraculously subsided. That never happens for me—my migraines can last for days. But that time I was healed. God healed me. And James left as quietly as he had appeared.

Later that day I asked the YMCA staff if they had an employee named James. I described what James looked like. I asked the people at the tournament desk if anyone named James was at the tournament. No one had seen or heard of James.

God knew the turmoil I was in, and by sending James to me He showed me in a very tangible way that He was going to get me through this. This knowledge gave me immeasurable comfort in my time of grief. I never forgot James and his reminder to "just trust Him."

CHAPTER FOUR

• • • • • • •

THE END

"Consider it all joy, my brethren when you encounter various trials, knowing that the testing of your faith produces endurance. And let endurance have its perfect result, that you may be perfect and complete, lacking nothing."

—*James 1:2–4*

I HAD LOTS of questions that needed answers. "Why didn't you tell me you weren't happy?"

His answer? "I did."

But I didn't buy it. I would have remembered that conversation. I just couldn't believe he would do this to me, to us.

Rob looked at me. "I love you. But I am in love with her."

So that was that. My husband no longer loved me. And honestly, he had made the decision to end our marriage the day he was unfaithful.

I had been struggling with Rob's indecisiveness and lack of response for two weeks. It was traumatizing, tormenting. I needed to come to grips with the painful truth: This was not the man I had married. I was no longer dealing with that man.

That night when we went to bed, Rob fell into a deep sleep and was snoring peacefully. I lay beside him, wide awake and being ripped apart. I couldn't stand it any longer. I had to get out of there.

I got in the car around midnight and started driving around town. I drove by the Cue and Ale, where it had all begun on the fateful day when I found my husband in that topless bar. I drove by our church, his office, his parents' home, his brother and sister-in-law's home, and homes of our friends. But as long as I drove, I couldn't get the pain of his betrayal out of my mind—how this knowledge would deeply wound our sons and destroy our family if we couldn't find a way to turn things around.

Eventually I noticed the gas needle approaching empty. It was around 3:30 AM. I was in a bad part of town. As I walked into a twenty-four-hour convenience store to pay for gas, I noticed the customers inside had bloodshot eyes and were stumbling around in drug-induced stupors. I got some stares, too. It was a scary place. But it would have been fine with me if someone had put a bullet to my head. Anything to stop the pain. My home was no longer my sanctuary. I had no place to go. I was desperate. I had to tell someone.

I dialed the number from a pay phone. My pastor answered the phone. I told him what was happening and he told me to come to their house.

As I approached their street, I saw that they had the porch light on for me. My pastor and his wife were waiting at the door. As I walked inside I could smell a fresh pot of coffee brewing. I felt safe. We sat down in their living room. Quivering, I told them my sad story. My pastor's wife handed me a tissue. They were both in disbelief. Before I left we prayed together and asked for God's help.

By now it was nearly dawn and I finally had my wits about me. But I had one more call I wanted to make before I went back home. I needed to talk to my best friend, Rita. When Rita answered, I apologized for disturbing her, but told her that I desperately needed to talk. She suggested we meet somewhere that would be private. I didn't care where. She chose the parking lot of the Black and Decker plant off Interstate 95.

When I arrived she was already there waiting for me. It was easy to spot her car as it was the only one parked in the massive lot before the sun came up. I crawled into her car and spoke the painful words. "Rob is having an affair."

Her immediate response was denial. "Carol, that's not possible. Rob loves you."

I told her that it was possible, and that he was having an affair, and filled her in on the events that had led up to the discovery. Talking was freeing, in a way. Up until that point I had been trying to wrap my mind around what Rob had done. I wanted to protect myself and those I loved from the emotional pain. But now that I had told my pastor and my best friend, I was ready to face the truth and the gut-wrenching pain that came with it.

We prayed together. It was dawn by then and I was ready to go back home. Rob actually noticed that I had been gone! He asked me where I had been, as if he cared. I told him I hadn't been able to stand lying there in so much emotional turmoil while he was lying there sleeping as if nothing was wrong. So I told him about my midnight drive and that I had gone to see our pastor and Rita. I told him we needed to go together and talk to our pastor. I was surprised that he agreed to do so.

THE INTERVENTION

The next day we sat together in our pastor's office, facing him across his desk. Rob admitted to his infidelity. After he told his story, our pastor spoke. "Carol is willing to work through this and forgive you. How much pain do you want? A little bit now, or a whole lot more later?"

Rob was silent. He pulled his keys from his pocket and said, "I guess I need to turn these in." He had all the keys to the church as the head of building and grounds. That gesture made me heartsick.

Our pastor listened and prayed for us. He didn't provide marriage counseling or offer any recommendation to save our marriage. As far as that was concerned, we were on our own. And I didn't know what to do next. So we left.

Later I asked Rob if I could pray for him. He said yes. When I pray for people there is typically some sort of reaction as the Holy Spirit reaches a person deep in their spirit—guiding, teaching, comforting, and convicting of sin. But Rob had no response. He was listless. It was like I needed a set of jumper cables to shock him back to life.

It was eerie, haunting. I felt like I was praying over a dead man. I had never experienced anything like it.

THE INEVITABLE

I tried everything I could think of to reason with Rob. That night I told him exactly what was going to happen if we didn't get the situation turned around. I started reeling off all the family occasions that we would never share together: birthdays, Thanksgiving, Christmas, Easter, New Year's Day, graduations, summer vacations, weddings, grandchildren, even funerals. I told him that breaking up a marriage is never 100 percent okay.

We scheduled an appointment with a Christian counselor who was highly recommended to us. We saw her individually, each sharing our side of the story, and since we met in private I didn't know what she said to Rob. When she met with me she gave me no advice about what action to take to begin recovering from my husband's affair, work through my grief, or emotionally heal from the trauma—let alone if there was anything I could do to stop it. After our initial session she didn't offer us any kind of plan to work on the marriage.

I felt like I was drowning and no one was throwing me a life preserver. I reached out to all the resources I knew of, but it seemed like there was no one in my community who was skilled in saving marriages.

I was completely on my own.

Gradually I began to realize that I was losing my husband and my marriage—and my way of life as I knew it. I had initially been in a state of shock and denial, which had gradually turned into sadness and disillusionment, but now I was beginning to feel angry. In fact, I had never felt that kind of anger before.

I instinctively knew that I had to protect myself and our children. I went to the bank, made a withdrawal from the joint account I shared with my husband, and set up my own bank account. Rob came home at lunchtime in a panic. "I just checked our bank balance and two thousand dollars is missing."

I told him, "I know. I withdrew it and set up my own account."

He said, "You don't trust me."

My response? "You got that right."

Rob looked at me and asked, "What do you think I ought to do?"

That was just weird. Why was he asking me, of all people, what to do about our marriage and his affair? But he had asked, so in my calmest, most businesslike tone, I offered my answer. I said, "It seems to me you have two choices. One, you can stay and work it out; two, you can pack your bags and leave."

He walked over to our walk-in closet, grabbed a suitcase, and began throwing his clothes inside. I just stood there and watched and didn't say a word. As he headed for the front door I asked where he was going. He said he didn't know. After the torture of the previous weeks, in many ways I was relieved.

THE TALK

That night Rob came back home to talk to our sons. He took them outside on the deck and sat them down around the outdoor dining table. He then explained to them that he needed to leave for a while, but that they could page him any time they needed him. They wanted to know why he was leaving. He explained that they were too young to understand and he would explain later when they were older. This was crushing news to our sons. They loved their dad. They asked where he would be staying. He told them he didn't know. There was a lot of confusion. A lot of tears were shed.

I could barely stand what this was doing to them, and doing to us. We were all reeling from the harsh reality of what was happening to our family. But the pain in their eyes did nothing to bring Rob back to his senses. It was awful.

I wasn't going to enable my husband by keeping his infidelity a secret and lying to my sons. I knew that if I didn't tell them the truth, they would feel betrayed by me. And I wanted them to know they could trust me—especially at a time when everything else in their world was turning upside down.

So while I didn't go into details, I explained to them that their dad loved another woman the way he was supposed to love me. They needed an explanation for why I was feeling so sad and angry. I wanted them to be clear about what was happening so they would not blame me for this horrible change in their lives. Or blame themselves.

The next day Rob told his parents that he had left me. They were shocked and angry. They told him that they could not work side by side with him in the family business knowing he was destroying his family. That was the last day he worked in his family business. He never returned.

Friends tried to reason with him. One very successful Christian realtor in town offered him a job and an apartment to live in and told him he would pay for counseling. But Rob refused. Instead he moved in with his mistress.

I began to tell my friends about the separation, including the fact that Rob had no financial plan to care for me or our sons. I was starting to get worried. I was a stay-at-home mom and had not worked for pay for over fifteen years. A friend who had also been through a separation and divorce recommended I make an appointment with an attorney to learn what my rights were.

I didn't want a separation, much less a divorce. However, on Mother's Day I met with Rob and explained to him that I was giving him two weeks to come up with a financial plan for our sons and me, otherwise I would retain an attorney.

Two weeks came and went. It was painfully clear that Rob didn't want me or the marriage.

THE LAWYER

A divorce attorney's office was the last place I ever expected to find myself. But I was going to make sure my sons and I were taken care of, so I selected the best attorney in my hometown. I sat quietly in the waiting area until he arrived. He introduced himself and escorted me back to his office.

I told him the story of Rob's betrayal and what he had done to our marriage. It was humiliating pouring out my heart, telling him how naïve and stupid I felt because I had trusted my husband. It was so much to confide all at once that I began to cry. My attorney handed me a tissue and looked at me with the most intense, yet kindest expression I had ever seen. He told me that trust is what marriage is supposed to be built on, and without trust and respect there is no genuine love.

He started gathering all my personal information—the names of my children, marital information, employment information, and all those details I never thought much about. He then began explaining the process of obtaining temporary spousal support and temporary child support. Much of the terminology and concepts sounded like a foreign language to me. I didn't even know what kind of questions to ask.

Before I left I was given a mountain of paperwork to fill out, and the assignment of obtaining the following:

1. Bank statements
2. Credit card statements
3. Vehicle loan statements
4. Mortgage statements
5. Credit reports
6. Household bills

7. Current budget
8. Future budget
9. Household inventory
10. Separate property and inheritance property
11. Insurance information
12. Tax returns
13. Safety deposit box contents
14. Will

It was overwhelming.

I remembered the pain I had felt when I lost my father. That was horrible. But facing the death of my marriage was far worse. Daddy left me with the assurance that he loved me. Rob left because he didn't love me. This life-altering experience would undeniably have long-term consequences.

I needed to prepare for life without my husband.

A LITTLE HELP FROM MY FRIENDS

My sister-in-law was really good with numbers and administration, so I trusted her to help me with the financial side of the paperwork my attorney had given me. We spent an entire weekend combing through all the bank statements. Instead of giving me the assurance and confidence I needed in knowing and understanding my financial state of affairs, the numbers told another story.

More deception and lies came to light. Multiple withdrawals from ATM machines all over town indicated that thousands of dollars were missing from a savings account. This special account contained an inheritance that I had received after my daddy's death—an account I thought was safe and secure.

The marital betrayal was hard enough to handle; learning that Rob had also betrayed me financially meant that I had not only lost my marriage and my future, but possibly my security.

Rob was served with papers and the court date was set. He never once tried to stop the process.

I had never been in a courtroom before. It was intimidating. I felt like I had an elephant sitting on my chest. When my name was called I went before the judge and placed my hand on the Bible, pledging that with God's help I would tell the truth. Fortunately the day ended with Rob being held accountable by the court to pay spousal support and child support. I left with a sense of relief and felt somewhat protected.

My church family, my in-laws, and my Christian friends were loving and supportive to me and my sons during this painful time. They opened their homes to us to share meals around their family tables. Friends would take my sons to play in racquetball tournaments. I had countless talks with girlfriends over cups of coffee. My sons were able to attend a Christian camp that summer through financial support from others. A friend offered her condo for the weekend so we could have family time at the beach. Several incredibly generous people gave us gifts of money to help us through. God's love for me was demonstrated through His people in tangible ways.

I continued to teach Ladies' Bible Studies at my church. The study that fall was a precept study by Kay Arthur entitled "Lord, Is It Warfare? Teach Me to Stand." It's ironic that during the study I broke my leg. But I decided I was going to live out what I was teaching. I sat on a stool with my casted leg propped up on a chair and told the group, "Satan may be trying to mentally and physically kill me, but he's not going to kill my spirit!"

I understood that the trials I was facing were not meant to break me; they were permitted by God because they would reveal what was in me. Faith is not faith unless it is tested. I continued to hold on to those words James had spoken to me: "Just trust Him."

My church had completed construction of a beautiful new sanctuary and had scheduled a dedication service. I was honored when my pastor asked if I would agree to speak for the occasion. Still in a cast, I was assisted as I hobbled up on the platform on crutches. Before an audience of nearly a thousand people I shared my story of God's faithfulness to me.

I remembered a scripture God had given me from Isaiah, chapter 54, verse 5: "For your husband is your Maker, Whose name is the LORD of hosts; and your Redeemer is the Holy One of Israel, Who is called the God of all earth."

God said He would be my husband. I was not alone.

CHAPTER FIVE

....

PICKING UP THE PIECES

"For I know the plans I have for you, declares the Lord, plans for welfare and not for calamity to give you a future and a hope."

— Jeremiah 29:11

NEEDED TO find a job. It was important to me to have some control over my financial security. I learned that my attorney was looking for a receptionist and thought I could do the job—how hard could it be answering a multi-line phone and directing calls to the five attorneys who were partners in the law firm? I interviewed for the job and my attorney hired me. And the job came with a significant perk. My attorney said that from that point forward he would represent me free of charge.

I loved working there. I was the first voice that desperate souls heard when they called up in a panic because they were afraid their marriage was falling apart. I understood their cries for help. I spent countless hours with clients in the waiting area listening to their stories as they waited for their attorney to escort them back to his office. I understood those stories because I had lived them myself.

At one point my attorney told me I should put a collection plate on my desk because I was learning more about his clients than he was! I remember one of those clients in particular. His wife was having an affair, but he said he loved her and wanted her back. I asked him if finding out that she had been unfaithful made him angry. He said sort of, but he loved her anyway. I knew this man was in shock and denial, and told him that he wasn't really angry. But that changed. Each time he called he sounded a little bit angrier. Then, finally, the day came. I answered the phone and the client practically exploded into the phone, "Where's my attorney?"

The trauma of a separation and divorce caused some clients to do some crazy things. One client told me, "There are too many people in my marriage—myself, my husband, and his mistress. And one of us has got to go and it is going to be me." Another client drove around with a poster on his car with the words: "My wife is an adulterer." The breakup of a marriage can cause temporary insanity.

MY ADDICTION

I made my share of mistakes, too. I didn't medicate my emotional pain with food or pills or alcohol or drugs or sex; my drug of choice was the phone. Anytime I received a bit of news that was hurtful to me or my sons, I would immediately get on the phone to talk to one of my friends. I was looking for encouragement, comfort, and advice, but most of all I needed prayer. And I was determined to numb my pain. If one friend didn't answer, I would go down the list until I found an available ear.

I tried to stay out of earshot of my sons when I was on the phone because I wanted to shield them from my pain, so I usually took the phone into my bedroom to medicate. Sometimes I would hide out in there for hours. And while my intention was to avoid hurting my boys, I was actually doing the opposite; I was hurting them by not being available to them.

Through all of this my sons lived with me full time. They had difficulty adjusting to their dad's partner and refused to spend the night there, but I still encouraged them to have a meaningful relationship with him. Sometimes I was tempted to use them to relay messages or ask them to play detective, but I used all my will power and refrained. I held my tongue when they made disparaging remarks about their dad or his partner. Sometimes it was hard keeping them out of the middle of adult issues, but I was trying to navigate uncharted territory, and despite some of my mistakes, I did my best to try to stay neutral.

Still, there were moments when I was not. In the early months of our separation my sons competed in a racquetball tournament on their home court. We learned that their dad was going to be there with his mistress, and they did not want her around. Together we decided that if the boys withdrew from the tournament, that would get their dad's attention and make a statement. Okay, I'll be honest here—it was my idea, and I encouraged them to withdraw. But it didn't help. It just hurt them and kept them away from the sport they loved.

My sons grieved the loss of their family as they knew it. They were going through a life-changing event just as I was. At one point I reached out for professional help for one of my sons, but the counselor told me I was doing a good job on my own and I didn't need his help. On the one hand it felt like a compliment, but on the other it felt like I was being led away from the help I needed as a parent. Everywhere I turned for help the message I seemed to get was "You're on your own."

So I did my best to help my sons understand the most important thing—that they were secure in my love despite our changing circumstances. They were my greatest asset and it was important to me that they remember that even though this was a hard time, we would come through it.

THE CALLING

Eventually the mandatory year of separation was over. Our marriage was officially pronounced dead. It was a warm day in June, thirteen months from the day Rob had walked out the door. My attorney and I made that walk from the law firm to the courthouse to attend the funeral of my marriage, otherwise known as the divorce hearing. Once again I put my hand on the Bible and promised to tell the truth before God. But this time I felt different. God had given me the courage and the confidence that I needed. I knew I was going to be okay.

As I walked out of the courthouse, carefully putting one foot in front of the other as I made my way down the steps, I looked up at the noontime sun shining down on me. I had the distinct thought that God had released me from my marriage and had set me free.

Some time later I arrived home from work to discover that my sons had received a surprise in the mail. It was a wedding invitation addressed to them. That's how we found out that their dad was marrying his partner. They did not want to be involved in the wedding, and I respected their decision. However, not only did it make me feel sad for them, but we all went through another process of grief.

I was now finally able to move to the final stage of divorce— rebuilding my life. I was ready for a fresh start, and for me that meant finding a way to move out of my marital home. It was filled with too many memories of my married life. And it was too much house to take care of. So for fun, my friend Rita, who was a realtor, took me on a tour of some local homes that were for sale.

I fell in love with a cute Cape Cod house. My sons did, too. So Rita, my sons, and I formed a circle in the living room, held hands, and I asked God if it was His will for me to have this home; then, if He had to part the Red Sea just as He had for the Israelites so they could enter the Promised Land, would He please do that?

Well, God said no. The house was sold to another buyer. God obviously had a better plan in mind for me. So while I was bummed, I chose to trust Him.

One Sunday morning I was dressing for church and that still, small voice—otherwise known as the Holy Spirit—ever so gently nudged me. He said, "I'm calling you into the ministry of Christian counseling."

Seriously? Wow! Really? Okay, Lord!

I felt so loved by God at that moment, knowing He had chosen me for this endeavor! My joy was uncontainable. I believed in my heart that God was using the gifts I had had since I had been a girl along with all the trials I had experienced up to that point in my life. Suddenly it all made sense. God was using them to prepare me for this life work. I was honored to devote my professional life to this calling.

At the end of church service that Sunday I went forward and told my pastor and he affirmed my decision and prayed for me. Shortly after, a meeting was held and the church members placed their vote in support of my decision. My church commissioned me into the counseling ministry and presented me with a generous gift of money to help pay for my education.

I started getting my personal affairs in order. At the top of my list was putting our home up for sale. I called a realtor whom Rita had highly recommended to me (we didn't mix business with our friendship). Word got out and before my realtor even had a chance to put a For Sale sign in the front yard, the house had sold! I also resigned from my position at the law firm to get ready to begin school.

I began to earnestly look for a school that offered a Christian counseling program that would be right for me. I had heard some good things about Liberty University in Virginia, so I made an appointment to tour the school and secured a realtor in the area to help me find an apartment for me and my sons.

But something happened that I had not counted on. When I arrived at the school, something just didn't feel right. I couldn't put my finger on it. The realtor and I spent the entire weekend looking for a place for my sons and me to call home, but there were no houses available except for some condominiums outside of town. We went to look at them. They were across the street from a cow pasture.

There was no way I was going to uproot my sons and move them to the middle of nowhere! They were not used to that kind of solitary lifestyle. So I headed back home feeling like a fool. I had sold my home, resigned from my job, and told everyone I was planning to go to Liberty University. I panicked. In desperation I called my realtor and asked her if I could get my house back. She said no, of course, but she promised to help me find another one.

Then I called my attorney and asked if my position at the law firm had been filled. Fortunately no one had been hired, and he told me they would be happy to have me back.

I learned an important truth from this experience: Never to say that I am going to do this or that, but rather to say "If the Lord wills..." God always answers prayer, and His answers come in the form of yes, no, and wait.

I couldn't wait to find a home, however. My boys and I needed a place to live, which meant I needed to find a home right away. I remembered how much I had loved that cute Cape Cod house that I had prayed for, and thought maybe I could find a similar house in the same neighborhood. So I decided to drive by, and as I turned the corner, I could not believe my eyes. There was a For Sale by Owner sign in the yard!

I made an appointment to see the Cape Cod house again. Inside it was not the same house I had been shown earlier. It was beautifully decorated with customized window treatments and gorgeous wallpaper, and it had been freshly painted. It turned out that the owner was an interior decorator, and it definitely showed. I put an offer on the house and within thirty days it was mine.

I realized that when I thought God had said no to my earlier prayer for the house, He had in fact told me to wait. He knew what my future held. And when it was time, the house was more beautiful than ever. He really showed off that time!

THE PATH

One Saturday I was shopping at a department store and ran into a friend from church. He had recently finished his master of divinity program and had been ordained as a pastor. I explained to him that I had been looking for a school so I could get my master's in Christian counseling.

He said, "Carol, I think I know just the school for you. Have you visited Southeastern Seminary in Wake Forest, North Carolina? They have a counseling program and I think you would love it."

It had never crossed my mind to attend a seminary, but I took his advice and scheduled a time to visit the campus—and it was just beautiful. There were large magnolia trees, gorgeous flower gardens, and brick sidewalks connecting the classroom buildings. The centerpiece of the campus was stately Binkley chapel.

After meeting with one of the advisors, I knew I had found the school for me. It was the perfect fit. I applied at the end of that fall and was accepted to begin the spring semester. I enrolled as a commuting student.

Everything was falling into place for me to begin my education. My oldest son Brent was away at college. Chad and Jordan were in high school. I planned for "school nights" in the middle of the week so we could have dinner as a family, and after the dishes were done I would drive an hour and a half to the seminary and stay the night in the commuters' dorm. Thankfully I had friends who lived near us and offered to look in on my sons and drop them off at school on the mornings when I was away. This would allow me to take a morning class and an early afternoon class and return home by the time my sons ended their school day.

One afternoon I went out to check the mailbox as I did every day when I arrived home after work, except that day was not like every other day. Inside was an envelope addressed to me and stuffed with a bunch of money orders that, when added up, equaled the exact amount of money I needed to pay for my first semester tuition!

I was overwhelmed with gratitude and awe. It was just another confirmation that I was following God's plan for my life.

CHAPTER SIX

· · · · · · · ·

BACK TO SCHOOL

"God sees not as man sees, for man looks at the outward appearance, but the LORD looks at the heart."

—*1 Samuel 16:7*

M Y CLASS SCHEDULE was set. For my first semester I decided I just wanted to get my feet wet. My major, Christian counseling, had both the theological side and the counseling side, so I registered for one class from each side—Introduction to the Old Testament and Pastoral Care and Counseling. And that was it—I was back in school.

Looking around the classrooms I noticed a few things. I was about the same age as my professors, the majority of the students were male, and I was old enough to be my classmates' mother! I quickly learned that seminary was different from a secular university. There were no fraternities or sororities or athletic events to attend. For the most part, obtaining an education to serve God in full-time service was serious business. Most of those seeking an education in seminary were called to serve as a pastor or to work as a career missionary.

As I reviewed the course syllabuses, one thing was consistent—I was going to be writing a lot of papers. Thank goodness I no longer had to type on my old baby-blue portable manual typewriter from the '70s that I used back in undergraduate school. Now I had a computer—and a whole new learning curve to deal with. I knew how to send an email and create a simple document, but that was about the extent of my technology prowess. I felt very intimidated. Scared might be a better word.

Not only was I getting back into the saddle with studying, but now I was going to have to learn the Turabian style of established guidelines for writing academic papers. There was actually a manual to follow with certain rules, expectations, and formatting consistencies for citing, quoting, and referencing sources. I also had to learn how to set margins, how to write a bibliography, and where to place footnotes along with all those computer skills I did not have.

I had to learn everything from scratch. And I definitely had to learn it, or there would be a serious negative effect on my grades. Thank goodness for Patricia.

I was sitting outside class one day on one of the many benches on campus. Patricia came up to me and struck up a conversation. I learned she was just one semester ahead of me, and told her how I was just getting started in seminary. Patricia kindly offered to teach me how to navigate the library, show me how to use the microfiche reader, and even give me some samples of papers she had written. A godsend.

I loved my Old Testament professor. He had this baritone voice like I imagined God would sound. To this day I remember something very powerful my professor said in class: "When God has a call on your life, the only way out is death." Coming out in that booming voice it sounded like God himself was speaking!

One day he was teaching about covenant between God and mankind. Covenant in scripture is a solemn, binding agreement between two parties, never to be broken. It is a lifelong relationship. He was relating God's covenant with mankind to marriage. The general idea in marriage is that the husband and wife establish a bond and stick together like two sheets of paper that are glued together so they make one sheet. They become one.

My professor went on to explain that God wants an exclusive relationship with us just like marriage is to be exclusive. God never breaks covenant, nor should a husband and wife break their marriage covenant.

Having heard this, I couldn't help feeling curious as to what my professor thought about divorce. So after class I met with him. I explained my story and told him my husband had left me for another woman. He looked at me with great compassion and concern and said, "Can't you go back and try to reconcile with your husband?"

With a puzzled look on my face I said, "No! He has remarried!"

My professor went silent. He had no idea how hard I had tried to make my marriage work and avoid an unwanted divorce. I could see the struggle in his eyes that said how painfully difficult it was to accept that my marriage could not be rehabilitated.

THE EXEGESIS

When I entered my second semester I took more counseling courses, while in theology I moved to Introduction to the New Testament. My professor was highly intellectual; he not only taught the New Testament, he also taught Greek. Part of the requirement for passing his course was to write an exegesis. I had never even heard the word.

I learned that an exegesis is a critical explanation or interpretation of scripture—a full-scale analysis of biblical text. It started with an introductory paragraph explaining what I believed was the central focus of the passage and my thesis statement. Then I had to fit in my argument about the biblical teaching, and finish with my own observations and personal application of the passage.

I asked the professor if he had any sample exegeses that I could look at so I could get an idea of how to write this thing I had never even heard of! Thankfully he was more than happy to show me some examples.

I chose to write my exegesis on Luke 15, verses 11 through 32, which is the well-known story of the prodigal son. I was intrigued by this magnificent story of a son gone astray, his father's compassion, and the elder son's resentfulness. This passage is all about God's divine love, which contains all the power to transform the most wayward and hardened heart. It definitely spoke to me.

At the end of my paper I wrote that my goal in my life's journey, especially in regards to counseling, was to be like the compassionate father welcoming home the lost and offering compassion to those who turned back to God. In doing so, I would truly reflect Christ's transforming love.

When my paper was graded and returned to me, I slipped it into my book bag. I wanted to look at my grade in the privacy of my room in the commuters' dorm—I was too afraid to do it in public! My heart was racing as I reached for my paper back at the dorm. I had worked hard on my assignment, but I still had no idea if the work I had put in was satisfactory. As I turned the pages to the back page, there was it was: 100—A. And a note from my professor with the words "Wow! Thank you!"

I bent over at the foot of my bed and dropped to the floor in humility, weeping with thanksgiving to God. Surely I was in the right place at this time in my life.

I was sailing through all my counseling courses. I loved my classes. They felt as natural as breathing, and I was making high scores on my papers and exams. I also noticed something interesting about myself. In my undergraduate days I would hide in the back of the classroom where I couldn't be seen. Now, in my master's program, I would choose the first seat in the front of the class. I was confident and highly motivated.

We learned about premarital counseling and dealing with problems within a marriage, but I noticed that specific instruction for helping people prevent or recover from a divorce was not an integral part of the curriculum. It was as though that problem did not exist for Christian couples.

And it seemed that I kept facing this same dilemma at every turn. I had no idea what kind of help was supposed to be offered for an individual or couple facing this kind of crisis. I couldn't find it when I needed it, and now, in my counseling program, I was not being taught a definitive counseling plan in regards to divorce. Given my experiences, that just didn't feel right.

THE DECISION

My oldest son Brent was at East Carolina University, Chad was a senior in high school, and Jordan was a sophomore. I was approaching the halfway mark of my own education at the seminary, which posed a problem. The limited times when the classes I needed to take were offered were going to make it difficult to commute back and forth. I knew that we needed to move closer to the school. And naturally I had some concerns.

Since Chad had six weeks until high school graduation, I knew he would be okay. Jordan was the one I was worried about. Moving away from the town he grew up in would impact him the most, so I wanted him to have some input in the decision. I sat down with Jordan and explained the situation and asked him to pray about this decision. I waited a week but he didn't talk to me about it. It took every ounce of self-control I had not to badger him.

I was driving Jordan to the sports center for racquetball practice the following Friday and finally I asked him if he had made a decision about a move to North Raleigh. He answered, "Mom, there is nothing here for us. Let's do it."

Relief swept over me and shouts of hallelujah came forth! Jordan had given me his blessing. We were a team.

Our house sold immediately, so I began in earnest to look for an apartment for us. I found a lovely apartment in a great complex, but thought there was no way I could afford it. Still, I took a chance. Much to my surprise they lowered the rent and the apartment was mine.

It couldn't have been in a better location. Across the street was a YMCA where Jordan could continue to play racquetball. His high school was two blocks away on the same side of the street. The seminary campus was a seven-minute drive from our new home. Chad was even planning to attend the local community college.

DR. CARSON

The seminary offered mission trips for the students to take part in. I really wanted to have this experience. In fact, I even bought suitcases in advance so that one day I could use them for that purpose.

One of the requirements for going on one of these trips was to raise the money to go. I also had to ask prayer warriors for support while I was away on a short-term mission trip. It was humbling to ask for money, but I wanted to go more than my pride wanted to hold me back. So I asked, and much to my surprise the money started coming in—so much money that I had enough left over to go on a second mission trip.

My first trip was to the Canary Islands off the coast of Africa. My friend Patricia went, too. She spoke Spanish fluently, which is the native language of the islands. Together we were a team. She interpreted for me when we were on the streets evangelizing, and also when I was the guest speaker at a ladies' group.

The second trip was to Prague, Czech Republic. The professor who taught my Introduction to Missions class actually came from Prague, and headed up that trip. He interpreted for me when I spoke to the students in the schools.

As much as I had wanted to go on these trips, the experience was more than I ever could have imagined. A love for travel and for working with people from different cultures began to take root. God put this love for evangelism in my heart—and little did I know He had bigger plans for me much later down the road.

I was now working as an assistant to Dr. Logan Carson, who was the seminary's distinguished professor of Christian doctrine. Dr. Carson was a man of tremendous faith who also happened to be blind from birth. So wherever Dr. Carson went, there I was, his arm entwined with mine. I administered his exams, read his students' research papers to him, and was his grader. He became my mentor, my friend, and a father figure. He knew the Bible inside and out, and could quote scripture and tell you where to find it in a skinny minute. He also made up some words of his own, like "shackerosity" (couples who live together), "tadpoles" (young pastors-to-be), and "teeneries" (female students).

For such a distinguished man, Dr. Carson was also a lot of fun to be around. In chapel services he would shout out, "Now that's the way!" when a speaker said something he liked. Clearly, he was not inhibited in the least, which allowed us to have some electrically charged discussions.

One time he totally misunderstood me about something, and no matter what I said, I just couldn't get him to understand. I actually got furious with him—and it takes a lot for me to get furious. I told him I had to leave the office before I would say something I regretted. I headed across the lawn over to the chapel and sat on the steps. And I started thinking, *"Wait. This is crazy! Here I am having an argument with a seminary professor who is also a pastor!"*

I headed back to the office, opened the door, and said, "I'm back." Dr. Carson was sitting quietly on the sofa in his office. He stood up—every bit of his six-foot-two-inches tall. Then he knelt down on his knees and lowered himself, stretching out on the floor with his face to the floor. He lay prostrate before me and asked me for forgiveness for the misunderstanding.

I cried. I had never had someone be so humble before me. Dr. Carson was a true servant of God.

THE DILEMMA

As I moved into my final year of seminary I continued taking the required theology and counseling courses, and many of those counseling courses moved into the area of marriage and family. This was the area that I had hoped to work in, given my previous experiences. But that's also where something happened that I was not prepared for. In my Foundations of Marriage and Family course we were required to write an essay on our position on divorce and remarriage. For the first time I was exposed to the fact that divorce and remarriage was (and still is) a hotly debated issue in the church. There were varied positions on the issue, and those led to disagreement, even among the faithful. However, there was no disputing my professor's position on the subject: No divorce, no remarriage— for any reason.

Suddenly I was faced with a dilemma. I knew that I could easily write an essay based on his position and receive an A. The problem was that I did not hold to his position. I was facing a crisis. Should I write for the grade, or should I be true to myself and risk a lower grade?

In the imperfect world in which we live, there are marriages that have been broken by divorce. And in my many years of teaching Bible study and being part of a church family, I had been taught there are instances in which divorce is permitted. Now I was faced with an entirely different opinion: No divorce, no remarriage—for any reason.

There was no one I trusted more than Dr. Carson—and I definitely needed his guidance now! So we talked about the Bible and how it is not silent on the topic of divorce. And I decided to write the essay according to what I believed the Lord of my conscience had given me.

As you might imagine, the essay I wrote was no ordinary, run-of-the-mill essay! I spent an inordinate amount of time on it. I researched the topic and provided footnotes and a selected bibliography, none of which were required. I backed up my position with commentaries and resources written by other biblical scholars stating that the Bible permits divorce in the case of adultery and desertion, and allows the mistreated partner to remarry.

I got a B. My professor thanked me for my essay, stated that it was interesting, that my argument was consistent, and that I had obviously researched it and worked hard on it. But was that all?

No! He had written comments disputing my argument all over my essay in red ink. And at the end of all those comments he suggested I come in and talk about the essay with him.

I was sitting on a settee after class with Patricia when my professor came up to me. He pointed me out. "You're Carol."

I responded, "Yes, I am."

"About your essay?"

"Yes. You mean *the* essay.

He smiled. Then he said, "I would like to talk to you about it. Would you ask my secretary to find a time in my schedule so we can meet?"

I agreed to do it. He must have looked me up in the yearbook or asked someone to find out who I was. This was no small class, as there were over 100 students in attendance, so it had to have taken some effort on his part to seek me out.

So we met. I told him my sad story. I told him I was a devoted Christian woman who, in a perfect world, would never have chosen to divorce. But I had had no choice, and ultimately had to acquiesce to a divorce. I spent an hour and a half in his office talking to him about my experience. He shared with me that he had a loved one who was facing a divorce. He said she had told him that he would never know what it was like unless he experienced it for himself.

I agreed. I left him saying that I although I respected his position, I encouraged him to understand that those who go through an unwanted divorce experience an immeasurable amount of emotional pain, often followed by financial hardship; that divorce affects the children, concerned relatives, and caring friends; that everyone is involved in the firestorm. I asked him to be more compassionate toward the person than passionate about a biblical position.

I understood that although divorce was not God's perfect plan for me, it was His prevailing will. And at that moment, talking to my professor, I realized that God's purpose for me would not be thwarted. In all His dealings with me He had been full of wisdom, faithful, good, loving, and just. He called me into Christian counseling and He would use my life experiences, divorce and all, to help His people—despite the various positions held on divorce and remarriage. I would continue to trust Him.

THE VIP

As I got closer to finishing school, I decided to take a course in Baptist history during the summer session. I really don't like history classes. Never did. Still don't. So taking this five-day intensive course would get me through it quickly. The class began at 8:30 AM and ended at 9:30 PM, with breaks for lunch and dinner. *Intensive* was a very good word for it. A whole semester was packed into five days. I thought I was going to die.

A visiting professor, Dr. Richard Land, taught the course. He was kind of a celebrity in Christian circles. At the time he was president of the Ethics and Religious Liberty Commission, which was the Southern Baptist Convention's official entity designated to address social, moral, and ethical concerns. The seminary I was attending was Southern Baptist, so that meant it fell under the umbrella of the Southern Baptist Convention.

Not only that, Dr. Land had been selected by President George W. Bush to serve on the U.S. Commission on International Religious Freedom. I remember Dr. Land putting his cell phone on the podium and explaining that if it rang, he would have to leave class and take the call, because it would be from the Commander in Chief of the United States of America. (And it did ring during the course!)

During one of his lectures, when speaking on a personal basis, Dr. Land mentioned a loved one of his who was separated and was facing a divorce. My ears perked up. In my mind, if there was anyone who could settle the debate of divorce and remarriage, it was the man President Bush turned to for advice on spiritual matters! I definitely wanted to hear his opinion.

So after class I asked if we could meet, and he graciously agreed to do so. When we did, I mentioned that I had heard him state in his lecture that a loved one was headed for a divorce. I shared my concern and empathy and then stated that I was curious to know what his position was on the topic of divorce and remarriage. I'll never forget his answer. He said, "Carol, on one end of the spectrum, I have close Christian friends who believe that even the death of a spouse does not free them to remarry. On the other end of the spectrum, other Christians believe that a variety of reasons allow for divorce and remarriage." Then he told me his position. It was a matter of personal conviction for him.

It was then that I conceded that there were sophisticated arguments on each side—widely differing opinions on the topic of divorce and remarriage. However, I knew in my heart, debate or no, that God did not view me as a second-class citizen because I had been divorced. And I refused to be stigmatized by those who took an extreme position on the subject of divorce and remarriage. God was my refuge. I knew I would have to answer to Him regarding my position and the decisions I made in my life. My crisis was settled once and for all.

CHAPTER SEVEN

• • • • • • •

THE DATING GAME

"My beloved is mine and I am his."

—*Song of Solomon 2:16*

ONE OF THE strangest things about getting divorced after a long marriage is reentering the dating scene. At least it was for me. I hadn't dated since college, and suddenly there I was... back in the (dating) pool. Needless to say, there were a few false starts.

One of the first guys was a client at the law firm where I worked. He asked me out to dinner. I thought about it and decided, "*What could it hurt?*"

The next day I received a bouquet of flowers. Then he came to see me at the law firm. Wow, apparently he was really anxious for our date! He leaned over my desk and gave me his business card. If I needed to call him at any time before our date, he wanted me to have his number. The business card had—not so subtly—been sprayed with cologne.

It was too much, too soon. Not to mention too much cologne. It felt just a little bit creepy. The more I thought about Cologne Man, the less I wanted to go out to dinner with him. Eventually I used that phone number to break the date. I know it hurt him, but I knew in my "knower" that this was not right for me.

Next!

Bill was much more promising. It started as a casual conversation that led to a request for a phone number, which led to a lunch date, which led to our next significant date—on Valentine's Day. Bill took me to one of the nicest restaurants in town. We had a very engaging conversation and seemed to really connect on a variety of levels. I felt comfortable around him, partially because he used a normal amount of cologne!

At the end of our very nice dinner Bill invited me to stop by his house to feed his Labrador retrievers. He showed me around his home, which was not especially remarkable except for one room that I clearly remember. It was filled with memorabilia from his service in the military. I called it his "I Love Me" room.

The contents of the I Love Me room made me a tiny bit nervous. Before I ever thought about dating again, friends specifically told me, "Whatever you do, stay away from Special Forces guys—they are different." As Bill showed me around the I Love Me room and pointed out some of his awards, I happened to notice a highly decorated uniform and asked him to explain what each of the patches meant. I came across a patch on his sleeve and asked, "What is this one for?"

His answer? "Special Forces."

Oh no! I just looked at him.

He smiled. He explained that before he retired he had served as a physician for Delta Force, a highly secretive special operations group that specialized in counterterrorism.

Great. Still, I didn't heed my friends' warnings, and dated Bill anyway. And in the beginning of our courtship it was like "moonlight and roses," with Bill saying and doing everything to capture my heart. And he did.

As we continued to date, I found myself giving more in the relationship, and things began to shift. In those first months he showed the best of himself. But in time the real Bill showed up. Eventually he told me that I needed someone to sit with me at church on Sundays because he wanted to be out kayaking. I didn't get it at first; this was not what I wanted to hear, so I held out hope. But while I was in total denial, Bill was moving on and breaking up with me. It was hard for me to face that reality. I crashed and burned and had to go through grief all over again.

> Humpty Dumpty sat on the wall.
> Humpty Dumpty had a great fall.
> All the king's horses and all the king's men,
> Couldn't put Humpty Dumpty together again.

That was it for dating. At least for a while. I needed time to heal. One day I was out walking my Jack Russell terrier, Abby. (Although to be honest, it was more like she walked me.) Often when we would walk together, I would take that time to pray. It was the first of October, with a soft chill in the air. We had a certain route that we followed around the neighborhood. But this walk was different. I suddenly stopped by the curbside and began to cry.

I looked up to the heavens and through my tears I said the most heartfelt prayer: "Lord, You have been a wonderful husband to me, and I am very grateful for how You have provided for me—but I have something I want to talk to You about. It's not like You don't know this already, and I don't want to hurt Your feelings, but I would really like a man with skin on. Would You look the world over and find a mate for me?"

He was so tender in that moment. That still, small voice inside whispered, "Give Me three years."

My first thought was, "Is God going to change my mind—and is it going to take Him that long to do it?" It seemed like an awfully long time to continue to feel lonely. But then I remembered a scripture from Matthew 7, verses 9 through 11:

> What man is there among you who, when his son asks for a loaf, will give him a stone? Or if he asks for a fish, he will not give him a snake, will he? If you then, being evil, know how to give good gifts to your children, how

much more will your Father who is in heaven give what
is good to those who ask Him!

I was filled with hope that God was going to answer my prayer
for a mate.

WALT

I felt like things were going much better for me academically.
My life was on the path God had chosen for me, and one of the
perks of going to school at the seminary was that I was incredibly focused on my studies. Now I was coming around the bend in
the last year of my master's program. Soon I would be back out in
the world.

About that time my pastor's wife said, "Carol, I was listening
to *Focus on the Family* on the radio and a man named Neill Clark
Warren was the featured speaker. He was talking about a dating
service that he started called eHarmony. You ought to try it."

I went on the website and learned that Dr. Warren was a clinical psychologist who studied marriage and observed that the marriages that endured did so largely because of certain characteristics
that created compatibility and provided the potential for long-term
marital success.

Hmmmm. I hadn't done a very good job picking men on my
own. I was curious about how this eHarmony thing worked. So I
signed up.

The first thing I did was take a comprehensive relationship ques-
tionnaire. And comprehensive is an excellent word for it—it took
me almost two hours to complete! Once my answers were finalized,
the system would match me with men whom it determined would
be a good fit for me. The only thing the computer couldn't predict
was chemistry. I received several matches, but I held back. I made
a vow to myself: If a man was interested in me, I wanted him to
pursue me rather than the other way around. I communicated with
several men, but for one reason or another they weren't quite right.

Then it happened. I opened up my email. "Walter from Kingston, Massachusetts, wants to communicate." I read Walter's profile. His occupation was IT manager for the Big Dig in Boston, which sounded impressive, although being from North Carolina I honestly had no idea what the Big Dig was. I thought it might be a radio station or something. I later learned that at the time it was the largest civil engineering project in the United States.

I was interested in getting to know Walt from Massachusetts, so I replied that I would like to begin communicating. And eHarmony made it easy to get started. The first step was a guided communication in which we each chose five multiple-choice questions to ask each other to break the ice. Then Walt and I exchanged our "Must Have" and "Can't Stand" lists of the things that were most important to us in a relationship.

It was amazing to me how similar we were. We moved up to open-ended questions, and that went well, too. Finally, after about a month of corresponding through eHarmony's system, we decided to throw caution to the wind and communicate via personal emails, with no more help from the computer geniuses at eHarmony.

My first email to Walt was a long one. I started by giving him what I thought was a cursory overview of who I was, and ended with some questions for Walt. Walt admitted to me that my email was a little bit intimidating. (Later he admitted that in fact it was so scary that he had initially wanted to back off. But part of the reason he was so scared was that he felt something for me—and he had been afraid of those feelings.)

I told him I appreciated his honesty, but I hoped he would continue to correspond with me. He did.

Another month went by filled with emails flying back and forth. Then Walt was ready to take our courtship to the next level. He suggested he call me so we could talk. I remember that first call. I was really nervous and excited. The phone rang at 7:00 PM—right on time. When I heard Walt's voice, I really liked it. He sounded gentle and sincere, without that southern drawl I was used to. Our conversation was so comfortable that we talked past the eHarmony-recommended fifteen minutes. Then Walt suggested we end the call in prayer. I really liked that.

That one phone call led to many more. It turned out we could spend hours on the phone. We would do just about everything together during those conversations—we would go shopping on the phone, cook on the phone, and even eat together on the phone! It probably won't surprise you that our longest phone call was about six hours.

During that time Walt told me about his spreadsheet. As an IT guy, it was only natural for Walt to create a special spreadsheet to evaluate his potential matches, weighing their answers to his most important questions. One key question was essential: "Do you believe your mate should be your best friend?" It was on his "Must Have" list. Out of thirty matches, only three women said yes. I was one of the three.

One evening we were on the phone (as usual) sharing our favorites, including our favorite color to our favorite candy bar and everything in between. We talked about our childhoods, our personal beliefs, our most embarrassing moments, our dreams, our thoughts on money and romance... even our pet peeves.

During that call we realized how alike we were and how much fun we had together—even if it was just on the phone! We never tired of each other. Feeling our relationship progressing, Walt mentioned that maybe in the next couple of months, after a trip he had planned to see his son in Alaska, he could fly down to North Carolina to meet me.

I got quiet. Deep down inside I was becoming emotionally involved with Walt. And I knew in my heart that I couldn't wait two more months to meet him. I needed that meeting to happen soon so I could find out whether or not I could completely open my heart to him and where our relationship was headed.

Walt asked me what was wrong. I gathered up all the courage I had and told him I didn't think I could wait that long. I told him what I was thinking.

Walt immediately got on his computer and started looking for flights to North Carolina. My heart began to sing! We talked about weekends that might work and settled on Mother's Day weekend. He was concerned about the timing, but I told him it would work out fine.

THE MEETING

Well, at least I hoped it would work out fine, because I had no idea what the rules were for entertaining a date I was meeting for the first time. Was I supposed to decide what we should do? Should I leave those decisions to Walt? It was all so confusing and scary! Finally I went to Dr. Carson to get his input. He would know what to do. He told me, "Carol, he is your guest. You need to make all the plans."

So I did. I told Walt I didn't want to meet him in the airport. I needed more privacy than a crowded airport could provide. So I asked him to meet me on the seminary campus. Walt had booked a rental car and a room at the Hampton Inn, and I had arranged to have a gift basket filled with all his favorite things (which I knew about from our phone conversations!) delivered to his room.

Finally the day arrived. I remember waiting on the seminary campus at the agreed-upon time, feeling very much like a cat on a hot tin roof. I looked at my watch and noticed Walt was running late, which was not like him at all! So I called him. I asked, "Where are you?"

He had been going through all the goodies in the gift basket and lost track of time! I was happy the gift basket went over well, but the anticipation was still too much. I was pacing in front of the chapel. And then, finally I saw a car pull up, and there he was.

I started walking down the brick pathway to greet him, my heart beating out of my chest. Then I noticed what he was wearing… and couldn't help but smile. He was dressed in leather work boots, jeans, and a tee-shirt. Walt now says that knowing me, he would have been better off in a three-piece suit, carrying a briefcase. But at the time, seeing my IT guy in his safe, approachable IT attire was exactly what I needed.

As I finally greeted him, he reached out for my hands and prayed over our time together. Then he kissed me lightly. The ultimate gentleman.

All of my feelings of nervousness were replaced by a warm feeling of comfort and safety. I showed him around the seminary campus and then we walked into town for lunch at a little sandwich shop. We got lost in time talking, laughing, and enjoying each other—just like on the phone, but so much better.

I had made big plans for that evening—reservations at Winston's Grill, and two tickets to a live performance of *The Phantom of the Opera*, which I hoped Walt would love thanks to our eHarmony profiles, which said he loved the theater. The entire evening was magical. And very romantic.

The next day we drove to Fayetteville so I could show him the place where I had lived for the majority of my adult life and raised my sons. I took him to the Fayetteville Rose Garden, explaining that there was a special spot in a wooded area with a wooden bench that wrapped around a tree where I would pray and talk to God.

Walt suggested we go there and pray. As we began praying, the songbirds of the woods began singing louder and louder. I asked Walt, "Do you hear that?"

He said, "Yes, it is like they are translating our prayer into song." And as if to prove his point, when we finished praying the singing stopped. We looked at each other, stunned, knowing that something very special had happened.

That evening we returned to Raleigh to spend some time with my sons. I was introducing Walt for the first time, and Walt decided that he wanted to cook for the boys. So we went shopping for all the ingredients for a chicken Caesar salad pizza. My sons took their first bite and looked at Walt and said, "She's yours!" Which is why Walt now tells everyone he bought me for a pizza!

We had one more stop to make later that evening—I wanted to introduce Walt to Dr. Carson. We drove to my mentor's house and were enjoying each other's company when Dr. Carson suddenly made a request. "Carol, I would like you to go out to the car."

What? I didn't want to leave—we were having such a nice visit!

He said with more determination, "Go get in the car."

So I did. Walt told me later that the two of them talked about how Walt's marriage had ended, and spent some time discussing theology and doctrine. What Walt didn't tell me was that Dr. Carson also told him, "You are the man I have been praying for. In due season, you are to take Carol home."

That evening Walt took me back to my apartment. It was almost dusk, so we decided to take a walk through my neighborhood. Walt drew me close as he was saying his good-bye. It happened again; this time a wind came up and began swirling around us, surrounding us with the fragrance of honeysuckle. We both said that if we had not witnessed it for ourselves, no one would have believed it.

And then the evening was over. Walt's flight home to Boston was at 7:30 AM, so he said good night and kissed me good-bye. My heart was full, and I was sad to see him go.

THE ENDORSEMENT

The next morning I checked my email and found a message from Dr. Carson in my inbox. The subject line read: "First Water." I clicked on the email to open it. Dr. Carson had written:

"Walter is of the order of first water."

I had no idea what that meant.

Walt called me later to let me know that he had arrived home safely. I told him about the email and asked him if he knew what it meant. He didn't, so being the IT genius he is, he Googled "First Water." "First Water diamonds" came up:

1. The highest degree of quality or purity in diamonds.
2. The foremost rank or quality.

I realized what the email meant. "Dr. Carson gave me his blessing, didn't he?!"

Walt replied, "Yes, he did."

THE PROPOSAL

With Dr. Carson's blessing, we began talking about a future together. Then one day Walt called me and asked, "Which do you like better—yellow gold, white gold, or platinum?" I began by saying, "Well, in my former life, I wore yellow gold. I wear silver now."

Walt's response? "Okay—platinum it is."

I knew exactly what that question meant. Walt was looking at diamonds. I was ecstatic!

My birthday was in July, and Walt flew me up to Boston celebrate with him. But this would be no ordinary celebration. Upon my arrival Walt took me to his office, where he had some special gear. He outfitted me in a hardhat, gloves, safety vest, and boots. Why? Walt wanted to take me up on the Leonard Zakim Bunker Hill Memorial Bridge—the crown jewel of the project he had been working on.

So off we went walking through the north end of Boston toward this humongous cable-stayed bridge. I had no idea what we were doing. Then Walt said, "Okay, we're going to climb up the scaffolding so I can show you the bridge before it opens to traffic." Thank goodness I am not totally afraid of heights!

We made it up to the top. Then Walt took his book bag off his shoulder and reached for something inside. He informed me that we were getting ready to do what few people would ever have a chance to do once the traffic lanes opened. I hoped very hard that Walt had not planned for us to go bungee jumping.

He hadn't. Instead, he got down on one knee, and right there on top of the bridge he asked me to marry him. He slipped a beautiful diamond ring with diamonds surrounding the band on my finger. It was gorgeous. I could not take my eyes off it.

And of course I said yes.

We climbed down off the bridge and headed back to his office, where he had a lunch planned for me at his favorite Chinese restaurant. His staff was there to help us celebrate. It was so special.

Later that evening we had our official engagement dinner in Wellesley, Massachusetts, at The Blue Ginger Restaurant. Walt had reserved a special table for our celebration, which culminated when the owner and chef, Ming Tsai, who is also an Emmy Award-winning host on the Food Network, presented us with a bottle of champagne for our celebration. The entire evening was enchanting.

We set our wedding date for June a year later. Now that I was an adult, and a professional counselor at that, I knew there were several steps we needed to take to prepare for the reality of marriage. eHarmony had already done a lot of the work for us by determining that we were compatible—something more couples than you might think have a problem with. Now that we were planning to spend the rest of our lives together, our last step was to work through a very comprehensive premarital counseling plan face to face to make sure that happily-ever-after was possible.

We obtained workbooks that covered every aspect of our backgrounds—familial, educational, vocational, marital, medical, personal, religious, and sexual. Some of the questions we answered were very private and sensitive—but we labored through the exercises with grace and understanding, and a little bit of humor! We both revealed additional information about ourselves including habits, likes, dislikes, and future dreams, as well as our failures and areas in which we needed personal growth.

The process allowed us to lay down a solid foundation of honesty. We knew neither of us was left with a false impression of the other. Walt and I were satisfied that we had met the criteria needed for a strong, healthy marriage. But just to be sure, Dr. Carson also provided us with premarital counseling sessions.

The year passed in a whirl as Walt and I continued to fly back and forth and get to know each other better while enjoying a host of recreational activities. We boated, fished, beach-combed, toured museums, cooked, and went skiing. Our relationship grew closer and closer.

COLD FEET

Soon it was March. Only three months left until our wedding day! But something unexpected happened. Paralyzing fear overtook me. I thought about my seventeen-year marriage and how it had failed. I thought I had been a good wife and mother. Of course I had made mistakes, but never did I think my husband would leave me for another woman. Why had I been not enough? And if I was not enough then, what made me think I would be enough now?

My mind was full of worry. I worried about how I would handle the transition of moving away from my sons, family, and friends to a completely different area of the country where I knew no one except Walt. And suddenly I remembered God's promise of giving me a mate in three years. I was going ahead of Him. I had not waited three years. Walt and I had rushed things. I panicked and became the runaway bride. I told Walt I was not ready to get married, and sent the ring back.

But Walt was patient. He had witnessed the event in the garden when the birds sang. He remembered how the wind enveloped us. He did not lose hope in us. He handled this hurdle like the gentleman he is. He gave me my space, but kept the lines of communication open. This endeared me even more to him—and his enduring love built the trust that I so desperately needed.

Still, I felt badly about what I had done. One evening I was so troubled that I had allowed fear to overcome me that I could not sleep. I opened my Bible and my eyes fell upon a scripture from 1 John, chapter 4, verse 18: "There is no fear in love; but perfect love, casts out fear."

I knew my love was pure, as was Walt's love. We both had God's love within us, which allowed us to love with His love; therefore I had no reason to fear. I had all the love we needed for our marriage to last a lifetime.

I realized that I had come under an attack of Satan—a liar, accuser, and one who destroys. Satan wanted to destroy what God was giving me: a man who promised to love me to no end.

In June Walt invited me to Boston to attend a black-tie affair. It had been three months since we had seen each other. I accepted, and we had a lovely time together, just like always. The afternoon I was to return to North Carolina, Walt pulled out the diamond engagement ring. With tears in his eyes, he said he could not wait any longer. He needed an answer. Would I marry him?

Through my tears I said yes.

This time we planned our wedding date for October; exactly three years from the day God had promised me a mate.

TILL DEATH DO US PART

Our wedding day finally arrived. We had planned a destination wedding aboard the Caribbean Princess cruise ship. My three sons; Walt's son, daughter-in-law, and granddaughters; our parents; and family friends all arrived at Port Everglades in Ft. Lauderdale, Florida.

My dear childhood friend, Gail, was my matron of honor. Walt's dad was his best man. Dr. Carson performed the wedding ceremony. And for those friends and family members who were unable to attend, our wedding was broadcast live via webcam (as any good IT guy's should be!).

It was a gorgeous sunny day and the wedding was held in the chapel on the ship. After the ceremony we shared a formal sit-down dinner in one of the beautiful dining rooms. Every detail was taken care of by the ship's wedding coordinator. At 4:00 PM our guests disembarked and Walt and I set sail to the Caribbean for our honeymoon. Our wedding day was all we imagined and more. Truly unforgettable. But what followed… would be even better.

CHAPTER EIGHT

• • • • • • •

PARADISE

"Then I heard the voice of the Lord, saying, 'Whom shall I send, and who will go for Us?' Then I said, 'Here am I. Send me!'"

—Isaiah 6:8

THE RENTAL TRUCK was loaded. My car was on a tow dolly attached to the back of the truck. Walt and I were driving to Massachusetts together. I had packed a few select pieces of furniture and left the rest of my household possessions in the apartment so my sons wouldn't have to set up housekeeping. The boys were all in a good place, either working or preparing to head to college, so I felt okay leaving them behind.

I said my good-byes. On one hand it was bittersweet. On the other it was exciting. It was an adventure. I was starting a brand new chapter in my life. However, for a Southern woman like me, life in New England was a major adjustment. I remember going to get all of my documentation changed to my new married name, and the car insurance agent asked me what country I was from! I paused for a second, then realized that he probably didn't hear Southern accents very often. So I asked, "Do you mean state?" We had a good laugh.

Then there was this thing called winter, which I thought I had experienced in North Carolina, but apparently knew nothing about. And I nearly froze to death. Of course it didn't help that I had arrived just in time for the hundred-year storm—a blizzard. Temperatures were below zero. I remember the front door of our home was covered two-thirds deep in snow. Unbelievable.

But I knew I might not be stuck in the snow for long. Walt was nearing completion of the Big Dig project, and we would be relocating within the next year. That's why I had moved into the same home where Walt had lived with his former wife in Kingston, near Boston. If that wasn't awkward enough, she had also decorated it, and her style and my style couldn't have been more different. I like a traditional, formal look, but my new home was country to the core. After a while all those ruffled curtains, braided rugs, patchwork quilts, and tiny prints started to get to me.

So one day I gathered all the courage I had. I looked Walt in the eye and told him I felt like I was living at The Cracker Barrel. Thankfully Walt took the news like a man. And even though we would be leaving soon, the next thing I knew we were choosing paint, wallpaper, and window treatments. Walt drew up some plans and single-handedly turned a walk-in closet into an inviting bathroom suite off the master bedroom. It was a huge improvement, and made my time in Kingston much more comfortable.

In the meantime I applied for a position as therapy supervisor of a geriatric psychiatric unit at a teaching hospital of Boston College. I worked with art, music, and recreation therapists, and met weekly in rounds with the psychiatric nurse, social worker, and physicians, giving reports on my patient caseload. Most of the psychiatrists and psychologists were Harvard graduates, so it was intimidating at first.

I ran a couple of groups. Since this was a secular hospital, I couldn't work with patients from an openly Christian perspective, but I was able to teach Christian principles on topics such as grief, anger, fear, self-worth, and forgiveness. And if my patients wanted to talk about God and faith, they could schedule an appointment with me to talk about that privately.

Those groups were growing, and the patients really loved them, especially the relaxation therapy group where I played soothing music, used aromatherapy, and implemented a few other therapeutic methods. The group was a safe place where patients could feel comfortable, and self-disclosure happened naturally.

One day one of the psychiatrists came to me and told me how much better his patients were getting as a result of my groups. He asked me if he could come in and observe me to see what I was doing. He had been taught to sit in his groups quietly and wait for each patient to speak. In contrast, I engaged the patients conversationally on a deep level. I was able to get to their unresolved pain by gaining their trust through meaningful conversation. It worked so well, it even impressed a Harvard grad!

That spring Walt and I received an email from eHarmony. They were having a contest and were looking for success stories of couples who had met on eHarmony and wound up getting married. We decided our story would be perfect. We didn't win the big prize, but they liked our story so much they contacted Boston's *Morning Show* and we met with a film crew who interviewed us about our story. We met in Paul Revere Park with the Zakim Bridge, where Walt had proposed, in the background. It aired on TV the next April. The story line was "The Zakim Bridge Led to Romance." I still love watching that DVD!

THE MOVE

When fall arrived Walt finally completed his assignment on the Big Dig. Bechtel Corporation, the company Walt worked for, offered him a choice of two assignments. One was stateside, while the other was in Kwajalein, Republic of the Marshall Islands, home of the Reagan Missile Defense Test Site. The Marshall Islands, in case you don't know, are located in the middle of the Pacific Ocean in a region called Micronesia.

After all that snow and frigid weather, who could turn down the chance to live on a tropical island? We certainly didn't! Walt accepted the assignment of corporate information officer, and we prepared to move to a tiny three-mile-long, half-mile-wide piece of paradise.

We were told we would be provided with a furnished house, and we were given a weight limit for how much we could bring with us. After talking to Walt's predecessor, we chose just three heavy items—our king-sized mattress, a recliner, and a steel gas grill. We filled out the weight limit with housewares, clothing, and fishing gear. Since it would take approximately sixty days for our household goods to arrive on the island by barge, we mailed several boxes ahead of our arrival. Immediate necessities were packed into our airline-allotted two bags per person.

After a fifteen-hour flight with a layover in Honolulu, we finally began our decent toward Kwajalein. A tiny dot of an island appeared in the middle of the massive Pacific Ocean. As the wheels came down, my heart was racing. Walt and I embraced each other as we looked through the window while the plane prepared for landing.

Upon arrival at Kwajalein we presented our papers for entry and security clearance, our baggage was screened, and we were issued our island identification badges. We were greeted by our sponsor and his wife and were presented with fragrant plumeria leis. We felt so welcomed.

Our new house was unlike anything I'd ever lived in before. It was a "dome home." It was brand new and looked a lot like a giant, white Hostess Twinkie. It had rounded exterior walls and a covered patio off the back. It was situated on the north end of our tiny island, just twenty-five feet from the water where the lagoon joined the Pacific Ocean. The views were amazing. We watched gorgeous sunrises every morning and majestic sunsets in the evenings, all from the same spot.

Nighttime was like a spectacular light show, because the stars did not have to compete with city lights. Seeing God's creation in all its glory was nearly indescribable. *Heavenly* would be a good word.

Speaking of heavenly, did I mention the weather? It was eighty degrees year-round; not too hot and never, ever cold. We enjoyed the warm, sunny days; pristine, blue water; and white, sandy beaches with the lure of the palm trees swaying in the trade winds.

Living in paradise felt like being on a perpetual vacation—intoxicating. What we did on weekdays was what most people stateside do on weekends. What we did on weekends was what most people stateside do on their vacations. There were more than enough recreational activities to keep us busy. We enjoyed boating, fishing, scuba diving, and snorkeling. There was a golf course, swimming pools, fitness center, hobby shop, and bowling alley. We especially enjoyed the outdoor movie theater.

Since the island was so small, there were no private vehicles. We rode bicycles or walked. Families with small children had child trailers, called burleys, which were attached to the backs of their bikes. For those who were not so stable, there was the option of adult tricycles. There was also a free bus service for transportation around the island. And if you insisted on driving yourself, golf carts were available for rent.

Communicating with the outside world could be a bit of a challenge. Our internet was dial-up, and we used calling cards to place calls off island. There was no cell reception, so there was no cell-phoning or texting. We communicated the old-fashioned way, leaving messages for each other on answering machines. Our landline had two different rings so we could tell when a call was coming from on the island or from overseas; on-island was one ring, while off-island was a double ring. Let me tell you, nothing was scarier than getting one of those two-ring calls in the middle of the night. I always expected the worst—but it was usually someone who had just mixed up the time zones. Since we were a day and seven hours ahead of Eastern time, it wasn't hard to mess up! So I told everyone from the States to call any time after 3:00 PM EST. Except for the time difference, it was actually really easy for our friends and relatives to call because calls from the States were not considered long distance as long as they called on a cell phone.

Despite the exotic surroundings, Kwajalein was a lot like your average American small town. The population was about 1,000, mostly American contractors, plus Marshallese and other nationals. Some contractors were accompanied by their spouses and other family members. Some of those spouses worked on the island as well, filling what were called dependent-hire positions. The spouses who did not work were affectionately called "island fluff."

There was one general merchandise store, which was called Macy's, but is definitely not to be confused with the American chain! The selection was very limited, which could be frustrating at times. It was not unusual to go to the greeting card rack and find that the type of card you needed was missing. For example, I remember buying a sympathy card and repurposing it for a birthday card—which was actually funny.

There was a grocery store called Surfway that had three aisles, with fruits and vegetables flown in from California and Hawaii, and frozen meats. We got used to having a limited selection. Since we didn't have a car, the groceries were delivered to our home by van. To supplement our diets (and put that fishing gear to work), we caught our own fish, and soon our freezer was stocked with a bounty of yellowfin tuna, mahi mahi, and wahoo.

Rounding out the list of island services was a convenience-type store called Ten-Ten; a food court serving pizza, burgers, and ice cream; a restaurant called Café Pacific, which was buffet style; and Sunrise Bakery, which served coffees, pastries, breads, and cakes. There were also monthly themed dinners provided by the Mobile Diner, which were held at sunset on Emon Beach. Those were really special. And if we wanted to do something even more exceptional, we could book a private dinner on the beach for special occasions. We certainly weren't going to starve.

We attended church at the Island Memorial Chapel. There was also a bank, a video rental service, a salon, a barber shop, a travel agency, a laundry, a hospital, two bars, and a marina. Kwajalein High School and George Seitz Elementary School educated children ages six through eighteen, although some families chose to homeschool their children upon approval. We had local radio and TV through the Armed Forces Network. The local newspaper, *The Kwajalein Hourglass*, was free to the community.

We didn't really lack for much. Still, I had heard that for some people the adjustment to island life was extremely difficult. Living, working, worshipping, and socializing with the same small group of people had its challenge, which is why some newcomers to Kwajalein booked the next flight out the moment their feet hit the ground! Others felt claustrophobic and counted the days until their contract would be completed. Not us. We loved it.

THE JOB

Being the former sorority girl that I am, I jumped right into the social scene. I joined a group called Nestbuilders for women who were new to the community, which was designed to support and encourage us through the transition of our move. After introducing myself and explaining my background, a couple of the women recommended I meet a woman from Kwaj (short for Kwajalein) who was working on Ebeye, an island nearby that is fourteen hundredths of a square mile in size.

I had read about Ebeye before my arrival. Approximately 15,000 Marshallese people, mostly children, lived on this tiny island. Many of the Marshallese who lived there found work on neighboring Kwajalein.

This woman was getting ready for a permanent change of station. This meant she would be leaving Kwaj and her position would be opening up. After I talked with her, she said I would be perfect for the position and arranged for me to meet the administrator of the Ministry of Health.

Getting to this tiny island was unlike any journey I had ever taken before. A few of the women went with me to dock security and explained how we would board the ferry, which was an LCM-type landing craft like you might see in old WWII movies, for the twenty-minute ride to Ebeye.

I arrived at the Leroij Kitlang Memorial Health Center and met with the administrator, and after talking for a while I was offered the job as counselor and consultant for the school-based health-care program. This position was provided through a grant from the U.S. Federal Government.

I was elated! So many feelings and thoughts coursed through my mind and soul at that moment. Prior to our arrival on Kwaj, Walt and I had seen a movie called *The End of the Spear* that affected me deeply. It was about five American Christian missionaries who went to the jungles of Ecuador to evangelize the primitive Waodani tribe. When the movie ended, I began crying uncontrollably, to the point of having dry heaves. Walt had to nearly carry me as we walked out of the movie theater.

Now, deep in my spirit, I sensed that God was calling me to minister to the Marshallese people. It was overwhelming to me. I was so filled with honor, gratitude, and expectancy. I didn't know how He was going to use me, but I knew He was preparing me.

I thought back to when I had been accepted to my counseling program at seminary. Because my first marriage had ended in divorce, I had to a fill out what was called a Separation and Divorce Form and attach copies of the complaint and divorce action. The form stated that the seminary would provide me with an academic curriculum, practical training, and any spiritual resources I needed, but I had to agree that my divorce might be a major impediment to ministry employment. And I would never be appointed as a career missionary.

That form was incredibly disturbing to me at the time. I couldn't believe that the mere fact that my former husband had been unfaithful to me meant I was disqualified to serve God as a missionary. But God reminded me that He had called me into counseling and He was faithful. He had a plan for me. He reminded me of the passage from Luke 18, verse 27: "The things that are impossible with men are possible with God." I was about to learn that again.

After the paperwork was signed, I began my new position. I had traditional Marshallese dresses made for me as a way to show respect toward those I worked with. Each day I rode my bicycle to the dock, made my way through security, and arrived on Ebeye with a short walk to the hospital. I was the only American employed at the hospital at that time—my co-workers were from Fiji, the Solomon Islands, the Philippines, Micronesia, and Myanmar, just to name a few of the many exotic locales that were represented on that tiny island.

To say that my workplace had a relaxed atmosphere is an understatement. Chickens and dogs roamed around freely. Children played on the hospital steps.

One day I heard music and laughter, wondered what was going on, and found some of my female co-workers dancing in the hospital during their lunch hour. They were practicing their *jebta*, which is a Marshallese dance. At Christmastime the churches on Ebeye compete against each other with an entertaining *jebta*. The women dress in matching Marshallese attire and perform these dances, which are very lively and similar to American line-dancing. Needless to say, I never would have seen anything like it at that teaching hospital back in Boston!

When I started work, my first challenge was to completely revamp the school counseling program. Prior to then, if a teacher saw that a student needed counsel, they would send the child to my office. But because the Marshallese are very shy and did not like to be singled out, I found this was not actually working. The concept of counseling was very new to the Marshallese, and something that as private people they just couldn't get comfortable with. I knew I would first have to gain their trust before they would ever come to see me privately. So I presented another plan with the idea that I would go into the schools and provide group counseling through weekly mental health talks. My hospital administrator loved the idea.

I introduced my new counseling plan in the public school and the seven church schools on Ebeye. With financial support from donations from friends and my home church in the U.S., money was raised for materials. I ordered art supplies, instruments for a rhythm band, and puppets to use in my talks. I worked with children from grades four through twelve using a Christian focus on topics such as self-worth, fear, anger, depression, and forgiveness.

Using art, music, and recreation therapies as modalities, the children naturally responded to this form of counseling. The teachers began to see a transformation in their students.

It worked so well that eventually some students felt comfortable enough to come to see me at my office at the hospital, where I worked with them individually.

I formed a friendship with one of the school principals, and after several months he asked me if I would consider teaching his senior English class. Their teacher was leaving in the middle of the school year, and he desperately needed a replacement. He went on to explain that even though they were seniors, many of the students were reading at a fourth-grade level.

Bear in mind, I was no trained English teacher. I had lived with one—my mother—but I didn't know a thing about teaching English. I told the principal I would pray about it. Then I went to the hospital administrator and told her about the job offer. She told me that as long as it didn't interfere with my job at the hospital, it was fine with her.

That settled it. I told the principal I would accept the position. We arranged for me to teach the class at 8:00 AM, an hour before my duties at the hospital began. He later told me that he had been praying for months for God to send a replacement teacher, and that God had shown him in a dream that He would send him a *ribelli* to teach the class. *Ribelli* in Marshallese means foreigner or an American. I was his answer to prayer.

But if I was to effectively teach anything, I needed teaching materials. So I sent a mass email out to everyone I knew looking for anyone who felt led to give to the cause. Once again, the monies came pouring in. My home church in the States became my mission partner in this endeavor as well. With their help I purchased an entire curriculum for the school, and I was also able to provide pencils, paper, and reading books for the twenty-five students in my class. They had never seen anything like them before.

From those who gave financially, I assigned each student an American pen pal. I explained to the students that we would be learning how to write a thank-you note. Their eyes sparkled when I taught them this skill. Then the day came when they were ready to address their envelopes. I had purchased stamps from the tiny post office on Ebeye and gave each one a stamp. They just stared at me. I wondered what was wrong. No one was moving. Then it dawned on me—these kids had never mailed anything! So I explained to them that they needed to lick the stamp and put in on the top right-hand corner of the envelope. There were so many giggles as they watched each other licking stamps. Then each student proudly walked with their thank-you note in hand as we marched to the Ebeye post office. The students handed their envelopes to the mail personnel. It was a sight to behold.

But that was nothing compared to how thrilled the students were when they received notes back from their American pen pals. They brought their letters to class and read them aloud to their peers. Some shed tears over their new prized possession—a personal note of love and encouragement.

MY MISSION

Most of my students had never received a letter before. Their lives were simple, and hard. The vast majority lived in lean-tos constructed of plywood, tin, and other such materials, cramped together with up to twenty family members or more. Sometimes they had to sleep in shifts. There was very little plumbing, so most of their families received their water from rainwater catchments or hauled drinking water from Kwajalein. Electricity was intermittent for those who had it at all.

I knew that with their limited resources many of my students would never get off that island. But I wanted to help them dream. I wanted to give them hope. Hope for today—and hope for their future, both practically and spiritually.

Each day we would have a "Word for the Day" with a corresponding scripture and a teaching around it. I also created a program called "Manners Matter," through which I taught the students how to have self-respect and how to treat others. They learned how to make introductions, and the boys were shown how to open a door for a girl and pull out her chair. I brought over dinnerware, flatware, and stemware, and my students learned how to set a table, when to put a napkin in their lap, when to begin the meal, and how to finish the meal. They loved it!

I ordered Christian novels for their grade level—similar to the Hardy Boys and Nancy Drew series. I taught them how to give book reports, speaking to an audience from behind a podium. When it was time to give their book reports, the students came to school dressed in their Sunday best. They took this assignment seriously! I swelled with pride. All the tools and skills I had been teaching my students were bearing fruit.

As I spent more and more time with the Marshallese, I began to learn their language and understand more about their culture. The Marshallese society is matrilineal, with mothers being highly valued and placed in the center of society. Land is tied to families and is passed down generationally through the mother.

Perhaps this was part of the reason why promiscuity was a major issue among the Marshallese youth. As I spent more time with the island's young people, I started to realize that sexual relations between males and females began at an extremely young age—often at the onset of puberty. That meant children as young as twelve or thirteen were sexually active, and many of those young girls went on to become mothers. In fact, it was my understanding that the girls were more aggressive than the boys. Pregnancy was an outward symbol of being chosen and loved.

The school's principal and I discussed this tradition. He told me he wanted to help the students learn and understand what the Bible says about love, sexual relations, and marriage. Culturally speaking, the Marshallese are a modest people, and the parents do not talk about sex with their children. Sexual discussions of any kind are considered taboo, particularly in the church. The Marshallese are a gentle people, and fear of embarrassment or guilt can be potentially harmful—sometimes to the point of suicide.

The principal explained how burdened he was about the youth. He explained that since I had earned the respect of the Marshallese and was in a position of authority as a *ribelli*, I could teach the youths what the Bible had to say about sex and marriage and it would be acceptable.

So I did. I arranged for a mission team of nine individuals from my home church to assist me with this endeavor. I spearheaded a five-day conference for the youths on Ebeye entitled "True Love Waits." We could handle 150 youths, and they attended in droves. Each youth received an orange tee-shirt with the words "True Love Waits—Takes the Island."

Suddenly the color orange was everywhere on that tiny island. Some of the students formed a praise band and led the worship. We had break-out groups with crafts, Bible teaching, and refreshments. At the end of the week we held a ceremony for the students who chose from that day forward to remain sexually pure until marriage. Youths came forward shedding tears of relief once they learned that they could say no to sex before marriage. It was culturally difficult to say no, but spiritually they learned that God's plan was to wait until marriage. I witnessed a miracle before my eyes. It was transformational.

Back on Kwajalein we learned that a new U.S. ambassador to the Marshall Islands was being sworn into office. The U.S. Embassy was at Majuro, the capitol of the Marshall Islands, and the new ambassador and his wife would be honored at a dinner to be held at Kwajalein en route to the embassy. Walt and I received an invitation to attend. Upon meeting them, I told them about the work I was doing on Ebeye in the school-based health-care program. The ambassador's wife and I connected, and we entertained them in our home on a couple of occasions after that.

During this time my co-worker Ei Ei, the physician in the school-based health-care program, and I had an opportunity to travel to Washington, DC, to attend a conference. But we had a problem. She needed a travel visa to the U.S. in order to attend because she was not American. So I flew with her to Majuro to meet with the consular officer at the U.S. Embassy. After we obtained her visa, I asked the consular officer if the ambassador was available. He wasn't, but my new friend, the ambassador's wife, happened to be at the embassy. She came out to greet us, and since we weren't able to meet with her husband at his office, she graciously extended an invitation to join them for dinner at their home. She said a driver would meet us at our hotel and drive us to their home that evening.

As we drove through the electronic gates with guards nearby, I thought I was on some sort of movie set. Our dinner was served on china imprinted with the seal of the United States of America. My co-worker and I had photos made with the ambassador and his wife with the ocean as the backdrop. After a lovely evening we returned to our hotel room and prepared for our flight back to Kwajalein the next day.

BACK IN THE USA

Then the time came for Ei Ei and me to attend the conference. We departed from Kwajalein and boarded the plane for the fifteen-hour flight to Washington, DC. I had the pleasure of introducing America to my co-worker and friend. When we arrived in DC she looked at the high-rise buildings and said, "So many layers!" She couldn't believe how tall they were. I loved watching Ei Ei take in all the sights. During our off time we visited the Lincoln Memorial and had photos taken in front of the White House.

After the conference, since I was already in the States, I extended my leave time so I could visit family and friends. I had been away for a year, and strangely I was having a hard time readjusting to the lifestyle back home. Call it reverse culture shock.

When I landed in my home state of North Carolina, I rented a car and quickly realized I had totally forgotten how to pump gas! There were so many steps... I couldn't remember them all! Then, on the road, the traffic seemed to go so fast, like everyone was driving at the speed of light. I drove at a snail's pace. Later, while I was visiting my sons, I needed to stop by a department store to pick up a few things. When I got inside I had a meltdown; there were just too many choices and too many aisles. It was overwhelming. I couldn't think straight. I turned around and went out as fast as I had gone in.

I tried going to the mall. People were too noisy and the restaurant music was deafening. I was suffering from sensory overload. But that wasn't all that was strange to me.

My friends had a meet-and-greet pool party for me, and since I hadn't seen some of them since my move to Massachusetts, I was really excited about catching up and enjoying their company. But something had changed. We were sitting around the pool and I suddenly noticed that everyone had a cell phone—in their hand, in their purse, sitting next to them on a table—they were everywhere. And every now and then they stopped to check their messages. A few people even got up to take calls. I thought to myself, "*Can't we just sit and visit?*" I realized how much I was missing my simple, tranquil, island lifestyle.

SPREADING MY WINGS

When I returned to the island, my life in paradise resumed, even better than before, as more and more opportunities kept popping up for me.

During a chapel service at the Island Memorial Chapel I was introduced to missionaries named Sylvia and Nob who were with Pacific Mission Aviation on Pohnpei, Micronesia. Sylvia extended an invitation to me to be a guest Bible teacher and retreat leader for the women of her church. I had years of experience leading and teaching women, so I gladly accepted.

Pohnpei was about an hour's flight from Kwajalein. Sylvia had arranged for us to go Nahlap, a lush, two-square-mile island on Pohnpei's barrier reef. We arrived by boat and slept in small bungalow-style huts. Rainwater was caught in barrels for bathing. It was pretty rustic.

Twenty-seven women were in attendance at the retreat. I taught the Bible study "Lord Teach Us to Pray" by Kay Arthur. We enjoyed aerobics at sunrise, fabulous snorkeling during our free time, and sweet fellowship at sunset. Lives were changed.

Back on Kwaj there was some talk going around at the Christian Women's Fellowship, which was the women's group at the chapel. Apparently there had not been a women's retreat on Kwaj in quite some time. Since I had had the experience of organizing retreats and conferences, I was asked if I would be part of the committee to make it happen.

We did it up right. We organized a two-day retreat. Our tropical setting made a luau theme the perfect choice. Each woman was presented with a lei when she arrived at the port of call. We arranged to have a sunset cruise on one of the U.S. Army's catamarans, where we served heavy hors d'oeuvres and desserts. I was asked to be the speaker, so I shared an inspirational message. We had special music. Two of my college sorority sisters from the States were visiting at the time and shared the occasion with me. On the second day we had sessions where the ladies could select a topic that interested them. The retreat was a huge hit, and an unforgettable experience for everyone involved.

Life in the Marshall Islands was as close to perfect as I could imagine. I had grown to love my job, and working with the students was such a blessing to me. I felt that God was really using me in ways I could have never hoped or dreamed of. I had become a part of their culture. I was invited into homes, sat on the intricately woven pandanus mats that covered the dirt floors, and comforted those who wept during a wake of a beloved family member.

Calvin, a co-worker and friend, was my translator for a Bible study I taught to the Marshallese youth. He invited me to attend his wedding at a private ceremony. Since I had a camera with me, I became the official wedding photographer. After the vows were made, a cooler was opened and we celebrated with sodas. That was the Marshallese version of a wedding reception. It was priceless.

One day Walt and I were reminiscing, and he recalled a conversation during the early days of our courtship. He had asked me if I had three wishes, what would they be. My response had been that one, I wanted to work in the field of Christian counseling, and was open to a variety of settings; I could work on staff at a counseling center, develop a counseling ministry, or counsel internationally. Two, I desired a helpmate with whom I could share my hopes, dreams, and future... someone my soul longed for. And three, I wanted the time and resources to travel abroad. Walt was witness to the Lord continuing to fulfill my God-given dreams.

GOOD-BYE

Unfortunately all good things, even God-given dreams, must come to an end, and our time in paradise was not exempt from this rule. Walt and I had been there for over two years, and his contract was nearing the end. When exactly that end date would be was kind of up in the air, which was particularly stressful for me. But eventually the day came.

No amount of planning could have prepared me for the shock and loss I felt when Walt told me he had been given the date. In two months we would be leaving. I felt numb. I was in a fog. One of my friends offered to stay by my side all day, and fortunately she didn't try to fix me or minimize my pain. She just stayed with me.

Thankfully we would leave after my students' graduation day. I had some money left over from all the donations I had received over the two years, so I ordered decorations for their graduation celebration. My students helped me decorate and everyone had the best time getting ready for this special occasion.

After an exhausting day of preparations I took the ferry back to Kwajalein to dress and shower for the event. I had been given a special Marshallese dress to wear that matched my students' attire. It was going to be perfect; I made sure of it. But when it was time to leave to catch the ferry back to Ebeye, I was horrified to learn that Walt and I had missed the boat! I caught the next ferry, but I was thirty minutes late to my students' graduation. But they had all waited until I arrived to start the ceremony.

I was asked to stand on the stage with the principal and the pastor. There were Marshallese dignitaries in attendance. I had arranged for an interpreter to be there so that all the Marshallese guests who were not fluent in English could understand what was happening.

I brought an American tradition—Senior Superlatives—to the Marshall Islands for the first time. I had even created certificates for the students from "Most Likely to Succeed" to "Best Smile." The students, parents, and guests loved the presentation. There were cheers and oohs and aahs. The parents in particular were so proud of their graduates.

After the ceremony my students honored Walt and me by giving us gifts of Marshallese handicrafts. The Marshallese women had prepared a traditional feast of fish, rice, corn, and fruits. We had so much fun that once again we missed the ferry—the last boat to Kwajalein had run for the night. This time we had no way to get home. Thankfully the principal arranged for one of the workers at dock security to take us back to Kwaj in his private boat.

The journey was terrifying for me. It was pitch dark, and the small fishing boat had no lights. I couldn't see my hand in front of me, and Walt and I held on for dear life. But there was no need to worry. The Marshallese know those waters so well that it was not a problem for the driver to navigate in the dark of night. All I could do was trust that we would arrive safely, and we did.

The company Walt worked for, Kwajalein Range Services (KRS), also threw a farewell party for us, which was held at one of the covered outdoor pavilions. It was a memorable evening. Words of thanksgiving and gratitude were offered to us both. Walt was presented with a framed aerial photograph of the island of Kwajalein, which included two Kwajalein commemorative coins. The photograph was signed by friends and colleagues.

But there was also a special honor just for me—one that I was not prepared for. I was presented with the KRS Presidential Award for service to the Marshallese people. I was very humbled.

MOVING DAY

The packers came and boxed up our household, securing all our worldly possessions (or at least Marshall Island-ly possessions) in crates that would be held in a warehouse at dock security for the next barge out. The barge would arrive in the States within two months. We left the same way we came—each with two suitcases in hand.

We said our good-byes at the airport and prepared for our long journey home. As the airplane taxied down the runway I wondered if this would be the last time I would ever see the friends I had made during my island stay. Among those who experience Kwajalein, there forever remains a special bond. And there would always be a special place in my heart for my Marshallese friends and students.

One thing I knew. Kwajalein and the ministry I had on Ebeye and beyond was a gift from God. He was faithful and I would continue to trust Him.

CHAPTER NINE

•••••••

HOME AGAIN

"Behold, I am with you and will keep you wherever you go, and
will bring you back to this land; for I will not leave you until I
have done what I have promised you."

—*Genesis 28:15*

N O MATTER HOW many times I had flown into Boston during our courtship, I have to admit that flying in over Boston Harbor is exciting. But after my experience of visiting the States while living on Kwaj, I knew the hustle-bustle of city life would be quite a contrast to our tranquil island lifestyle. I knew readjusting would take time.

Being back in the big city gave us a chance to do things we hadn't done in more than two years, and we decided to make the most of it. We toured all the sites we had enjoyed when we first met—Paul Revere Park, the Public Gardens, Boston Commons, and of course the Zakim Bridge, where Walt had proposed to me. We even ate at the Chinese restaurant where we had celebrated our engagement. Walt was able to enjoy all the accomplishments of the completed Big Dig project and feel pride in his achievement.

BACK TO REALITY

But we wouldn't be back in Boston for long. Our next destination was Frederick, Maryland—home of one of Bechtel's corporate offices. Until he received another construction field assignment, Walt would be working from an office in Frederick, supporting a nuclear project in Virginia. We had a month to find an apartment to lease, during which time we were put up in a hotel room. My view went from a turquoise-blue lagoon to a black asphalt parking lot, which was depressing.

Now the real readjustment began. We had to buy cars and furniture, since we had sold most of our household goods except for what we had taken overseas. We had left just a few items behind in storage.

Driving was a major challenge. It had been two years since I had been behind the wheel, except for that one week I spent in the States visiting friends and family. It took me a whole month before I felt comfortable driving by myself again.

Shopping wasn't much better. I could only go for short outings and had to limit my list to a couple of items, because the idea of shopping in a department store was just too overwhelming. I longed to wear my Marshallese dresses and shell jewelry.

Since I wasn't riding a bicycle for transportation anymore, I began my days by exercising to Leslie Sansone's *Walk Away the Pounds* DVDs. Then I would watch the clock until it was time to meet Walt for lunch, which was the highlight of my day. There was no newcomers' group for people transitioning back to life in the States. I felt out of place in my own home country. I missed my Marshallese friends and my island home.

Eventually I joined the Bechtel Wives group, which was kind of like the corporate version of a military wives group. We met monthly for luncheons and day excursions, and I especially enjoyed connecting with the ladies who had experienced an overseas assignment. They understood me.

Being back in the States meant that I needed to stock up on beauty supplies; I needed to find a makeup consultant. When she came over to share all the latest makeup products that had come out while I was living in paradise, we struck up a conversation. One thing led to another and eventually I began leading a Bible study with her. She came weekly, so that was the highlight of my week.

Walt and I went church hunting, but it didn't go so well. After church one Sunday we introduced ourselves to the pastor. We told him we had just moved to the area. He asked what kind of work Walt did, and when he found out he worked for Bechtel he said, "Well, you won't be here long." He then turned to the next person in line. Needless to say, we were disappointed in our reception there.

CLOSURE

But there were some good aspects to being back home in the States, too. A few months before we were scheduled to leave Kwaj, my youngest son, Jordan, mentioned that he had met someone special—Amanda. I always knew that when Jordan fell in love he would probably tell me that he had met someone and was getting married all in one breath. And he basically did just that.

They got married eight months later, shortly after we had arrived back in Boston. I would meet my future daughter-in-law for the very first time at their wedding. But I had purposed in my heart that I would love her, and it paid off. She's the first girl on my side of the family besides me, which definitely comes in handy.

Jordan's wedding brought me more than a beautiful daughter-in-law; it also brought me my first opportunity for some kind of closure with Rob. While the wedding preparations were under way, Rob called me and told me to let him know whatever I needed from him for the rehearsal dinner. He told me he trusted me and would just write me a check. That meant a lot to me, especially after what I had been through with the divorce.

When the wedding festivities began, it had been over four years since I had spoken to, much less seen, my former husband. It was then that I caught a glimpse of the Rob I had once known. When I saw him with our sons I could see in his eyes regret and sadness for the pain he had put his family through. He seemed to be fighting tears.

I also learned that his marriage had just ended. His wife had left him and he was going through the divorce process all over again. I was overwhelmed with feelings of compassion and forgiveness in my heart for him. I saw something in his countenance that my heart had longed to see for over twelve years, and it was balm to my soul.

Being back in the States allowed us to experience this, and to reunite with family and friends. For the first time in two years we enjoyed holidays and other occasions with our loved ones. We also took some side trips on the weekends. We couldn't do that on the island unless we boarded a plane! However, truth be told, nothing would ever compare to living in paradise.

We lived in that limbo for eight months. I felt like I was in a waiting room, but I waited with expectancy to see what God had in store for me next.

PARADISE... AGAIN!

The day finally came. Walt was offered the position of IT functional manager at three different nuclear power plants. His choice: Turkey Point Nuclear Plant in Homestead, Florida. Homestead is a city in Miami-Dade County at the gateway of the Florida Keys. We were headed down to a subtropical climate—and of course we were happy about it! God knew just what we needed.

We packed a rental truck with necessities, since our household goods were being shipped later, and moved into a motel room until we could find an apartment or house to lease. I found a realtor who showed me houses while Walt was working. But I noticed that most homes had chain-link fences around them, and the windows were covered with iron bars. I didn't feel comfortable anywhere.

One day I decided to drive thirty miles south of Homestead down U.S. Highway 1 toward Key Largo, Florida. As I crossed over the bridge at mile marker 108 I saw sparkling blue water and palm trees. My heart skipped a beat.

I drove around and looked at homes on both the bay side and the ocean side. There were lots of restaurants and a small shopping center with a grocery store and a department store. I just knew that this would be the perfect hometown. But I needed to convince Walt. Moving to Key Largo meant he would be commuting forty-five minutes every day to work.

That weekend we drove down to Key Largo. Turns out I didn't need to worry. Walt took one look and that was the end of it. We found a realtor and began house-hunting. One day Walt came home from work and told me about a Key Largo townhouse for rent that he had found posted on the board at work. It was in a private gated community called The Sanctuary. It sounded… peaceful.

We met with the realtor and we fell in love with it. The water-front townhouse was on the bay side, with two bedrooms and a screened terrace by the water. Some of the amenities at the complex included a swimming pool, clubhouse, gym, tennis courts, boat ramp, and dry boat storage.

We didn't have a boat. That lasted about five days. Walt's second love is fishing, so after we signed the lease, we became proud boat owners.

Life felt normal again. We enjoyed the subtropical climate and sunsets every night. But I didn't like being "island fluff."

BACK TO WORK

So I got on Google, searched the churches in the area, found a church on the mainland, and discovered the pastor had graduated from the same seminary as I had! So I gave him a call and explained that I had a master's in Christian counseling and was looking for work. He wanted to meet me.

The pastor indicated that he needed a counselor. There was just one catch—he couldn't pay me. So I looked into what I needed to do to start a counseling ministry. I met with the deacon board and they approved me to do the work. I shared my testimony before the church body one Sunday evening. I found out that I could provide counseling as a sole proprietor and come in under the umbrella of the church.

I had an attorney draw up an independent contract agreement. The church would provide me with an appropriate office space and I would perform counseling services. I cut my fee in half as a courtesy to church members.

I was really excited about launching my counseling ministry. The space that was offered was in the library of the church. I had been promised furniture, but until it arrived the church provided a white banquet table and brown folding chairs.

My office furniture never came. And there were other problems. Clients confided that they did not like being seen by church staff when they came to see me; confidentiality was an issue. Sometimes church members would come into the library while I was counseling. When networking in the community, I learned that pastors did not like sending their members to another church for help.

I saw whoever came through my door. I worked with children, adolescents, and adults. I helped clients with communication issues, family conflict, grief, depression, codependency, infidelity, divorce, anxiety, and issues of faith. You name the problem, I was there to help solve it!

I had reports of the work I was doing prepared monthly so they could be shared at business meetings, but I was never called on during those meetings. I requested that the church announce my services on the overhead on Sundays, or in materials, but they were not. In fact, on several occasions I noticed my business cards had been removed from the table outside the sanctuary.

At every monthly meeting I brought my concerns to the pastor. But it seemed his hands were tied, because nothing changed. I quickly saw that despite our mutual best interests, this arrangement was not going to work out.

I began to feel invisible. Finally, after eight months with no change, I submitted a resignation letter. Although I was not an employee, I did so out of courtesy to the pastor and the church.

I had tried to do the best job I could, but the conditions at the church made it impossible. Ultimately I realized that all I had been doing was following God's plan. Working at that church did not feel right because it was not the right place for me. God knew where that place would be. All I had to do was trust that He would lead me there.

SETTLING IN

Walt and I definitely enjoyed our Florida lifestyle. We found a church home and felt very welcomed from the moment we walked through the doors. We boated and fished on the weekends and went on an occasional day trip to Miami or Key West. But our daily lunch dates were a thing of the past. The nuclear plant was a lot different from Bechtel's home office, and I was not welcome there. In fact, only those people who were issued a badge were granted access at all. Walt had to go through explosive sniffers, metal detectors, and a machine-generated handprint and fingerprint access, and then swipe his badge. There were armed guards throughout the plant. No room for "island fluff" at the plant!

But our Friday night dates made up for it. We found this cute Italian hideaway below Key Largo in Islamorada. It had an outdoor patio with gorgeous fuchsia and purple bougainvillea flowers hanging from the mahogany trees. We would usually be the first customers on Friday night. In the back left corner was our table. Our waitress knew exactly what we wanted and would see us coming through the doors. Bucko, an old golden retriever who was the restaurant's mascot, would sit at our feet hoping for handouts. We would prop our feet up on the extra chairs and catch up on the week's events. The sun would set over dinner. It was the perfect end to a long work week.

Then I landed a part-time job with Hospice of the Florida Keys as their spiritual care counselor and liaison to the community. One day I was looking over the patient caseload when I saw the name of a patient I recognized. Her name was the same as that of my former neighbor in North Carolina. Our boys had played together, but we had lost track of each other over the past twelve years. Could it be the same person?

I took the chaplain aside and told him I thought I knew this patient. He told me that he knew her personally. I asked him if she had blond hair. He said yes. I asked him if she had four boys. He said yes. I told him that we were friends and neighbors and that I had led her to Christ. He told me that she had a tremendous influence spiritually on the community in the Keys and said, "Let's call her now."

So he called her and told her he was with a lady who thought she knew her, and asked if she knew a lady named Carol who had been her neighbor in North Carolina.

She said, "Yes, I know Carol!"

He told her I would like to speak with her. I got on the phone with my friend and the first words out of her mouth were, "Carol, you led me to the Lord!"

I said, "I did, didn't I!" It was a God moment.

My old friend had lost her sight in both eyes due to cancer. I needed her friendship and she needed mine. We caught up on years lost. She was an unexpected gift from God!

BECOMING DR. CAROL

During this time I started taking additional classes and receiving further training to sharpen some of my counseling skills. It occurred to me that I could pursue a doctorate in clinical Christian counseling, and I found an online program geared more toward ministry; it was a perfect fit for me. Inch by inch I completed all the coursework, and in the end I had to write a dissertation. I entitled it *Clinical Significance of Temperament in Christian Counseling*. It felt like a work of art, and I was really excited to get my leather-bound copy when it arrived in the mail.

My counseling program in seminary had focused on working in a church. Well, I had tried that and it hadn't worked for me. But I didn't know anything about setting up my own counseling ministry. So I contacted an organization and met their requirements to begin under their umbrella. They were extremely supportive and encouraging.

Of course Walt helped me build my first website. It was exciting getting that launched, even if it just looked pretty!

Still, I didn't know anything about the business side of counseling. That was something they didn't teach in counseling school, even in the Ph.D. program! So I looked online and found a woman named Casey Truffo who is a business coach who works specifically with counselors helping them build their practices. She offered a step-by-step online practice-building coaching program with weekly coaching calls. Realizing she was exactly what I needed, I hired her to help me.

I began to learn all sorts of things from Casey to help me build the practice I wanted to build. For example, I learned that I could specialize in a certain area of counseling and serve a specific clientele that was a good fit for me. That meant I could concentrate on helping people through the trauma of divorce, which is what I felt God had called me to do (more on that later!). I also learned more of the "business-y" stuff, like what to say when a potential client calls, how to set a fee, network in the community, speak, write a blog, choose a niche, and keep in touch through a newsletter.

The first thing I did was let my friends and family know about my new practice. And they told others. The next thing I knew, I was starting to get calls.

But I had a problem. I didn't have an office yet because I wasn't making enough money to pay for a lease. So I started seeing clients by offering phone counseling. Unfortunately our townhouse was built of solid concrete, and the cell service did not have a cell tower close by, so calls would drop in the middle of a sentence—which is the last thing you want to have happen in the middle of a counseling session!

Since service was better outside, my car became my office. I would take my laptop out there, turn the car on so I would have air-conditioning, and wait for my client to call. And I would sit there in the car counseling my clients from daytime to evening. I just pretended they were talking to me in an executive corner office in a high-rise building on Miami Beach. I learned later that the maintenance crew at our townhouse was worried about me and asked Walt what I was doing in the car all the time!

Over time I built my practice to the point where I could afford a shared office space. So I started talking to other counselors in Key Largo to find out if I could see clients during the times they weren't using their spaces. I was surprised to come up against a lot of resistance. When I told one counselor I specialized in helping individuals navigate the challenges of divorce, she actually said, "We don't have those problems here."

That one made me laugh! But some of the other rejections weren't as amusing. I had named my counseling ministry Pathways Christian Counseling, and one counselor asked me if I would take the word *Christian* out of the name. Another said her clients might be offended by my diplomas and degrees with the word *Christian* on them. It seemed like no one wanted to share an office with me!

Then one weekend Walt and I were out walking and passed a little strip of storefronts. One in particular caught my eye. It was a counselor's office that I had not seen. I scribbled the number down and thought I would give the counselor a call to see if she was interested in sharing space.

Rosanne was a godsend. She said she would love for me to come on board, Christian or not! So I hung my credentials on the wall and got started. It was an exciting time for me.

Soon my practice was filling beyond the point where a shared space could accommodate me. I knew it was time to launch my own office, and I found the perfect space at a complex of executive office suites called The Pink Plaza. There was an office available with windows across the entire back wall and a view of Florida Bay between houses—a tiny water view, but it was good enough for me!

I ordered furniture, woven blinds, and décor. I had a coffee bar and a small glass-front refrigerator with cold beverages. Every client who came through the doors I considered a blessing sent by God.

Since I was the only Christian counselor on the Florida Keys, I attracted clients from as far as an hour or more away. Individuals and couples came from north of Miami and as far south as Marathon.

My new office was located near an exclusive gated community called the Ocean Reef Club, which had its own secluded spot at the northern end of Key Largo. It was almost like a little private town, with its own private airport, which was probably why it was also home to many professional athletes and movie stars. I offered a special VIP service, traveling to the Ocean Reef Club to see clients in their homes, offering an extra measure of client confidentiality for couples who didn't want to be seen seeking counseling in public. And I became a counselor to the stars! (Whose names will remain secret, of course.)

Before long my counseling ministry was thriving. And more important, it grew away from helping people survive divorce. Instead I was becoming known for helping save marriages.

FINDING OUR FOREVER HOME

After two years at Turkey Point, Walt reached the halfway point on the project and starting thinking about retiring. We enjoyed having friends and family visit while living in Florida, but we also knew it was time to start thinking about a permanent home to call our own once the project ended. We knew we wanted to be somewhere warm and on the water. So Walt used the internet to "fly" over all the coastal areas from the Florida Keys to Charleston,

South Carolina. We had already looked from Virginia to North Carolina when we had driven down to Florida from Maryland.

Walt being Walt, he created a spreadsheet with all the features we wanted in a house. Ultimately we decided to focus on the low country area in South Carolina. There we would be close enough to family, but still southern enough to enjoy a mild climate.

We took a long weekend and drove up to South Carolina to begin our house-hunting. We had preselected the homes we wanted shown to us, and beyond that we spent our time in prayer. It was very important to us to be where God wanted us to be.

After so many years of renting, looking for what would be our "forever home" was a lot like looking for a mate. We had our "must have" and "can't stand" lists. We secured "matchmakers"—actually realtors—in three cities: Savannah, Hilton Head Island, and Beaufort. But when we went to Savannah and Hilton Head, nothing stood out. Beaufort was next, and it was different.

When we arrived and drove down Bay Street, our hearts leaped together. We looked at each other and smiled—Beaufort had that hometown feel we were looking for. The gorgeous antebellum homes surrounded by majestic oak trees with Spanish moss draped over their limbs grabbed our attention. We were surrounded by emerald-green salt marshes, home to a variety of wildlife. We had found our seaside town. Now we had to find our home.

We did some ride-bys and crossed off some of the houses that did not appeal to us. The next day we met with our realtor and looked at the rest of the houses on our list. Our realtor's boss looked at our list and noticed one particular house, asking: "Why is this one crossed off?" We told her it was too expensive. She insisted we go see it. So off we went.

As we drove down the private street, the low-country-designed home came into view. It was beautiful. Walt and I looked at each other with hope. When we arrived at the house, the first place Walt headed was down to the water to see the dock. It was covered, and had a sink, a storage box for fishing equipment, and a ramp down to the floating dock—a perfect deep-water dock with access to the intracoastal waterway. Walt said, "I'll take the house if the dock comes with it."

Of course, I needed to see the actual house to make that decision! Our realtor opened the front door. Since Walt is the cook in the family, the gourmet kitchen sold us on the place immediately. We loved the hardwood floors throughout. The house had been freshly painted inside and out and the water view was spectacular. We would finally have enough room to entertain our families. We knew we had found our home.

Well… almost. It was still too expensive. We drove back to the realtor's office and she and her boss began talking. The house was bank-owned and the bank was ready to move it. So we submitted a bid much lower than the asking price. And much to our amazement, our offer was accepted! Walt and I were overjoyed! God had yet again answered our prayer.

For the first time in our marriage we were proud homeowners. We hopped in our car to drive over to our brand new home. But before Walt started the car, I noticed we were parked behind our realtor's car, and the license plate had the letters *ERB* on it— our last name—a display of God's sovereignty. Nothing takes Him by surprise.

CHAPTER TEN

• • • • • • •

FINALLY HOME

"For we are His workmanship, created in Christ Jesus for good works, which God has prepared beforehand, that we should walk in them."

—*Ephesians 2:10*

I T WAS THAT time again. Walt was winding up the project in Florida, which meant we would soon be moving to our permanent dream home in South Carolina. But there was another decision to make. Walt had been offered a short-term assignment—nine months at a nuclear plant in Ohio. If he took the job, that nine months would enable us to meet all our financial goals, and Walt could retire.

I had no plans to retire any time soon. In fact, in my mind the only way I would ever stop doing what I do would be when the last shovelful of dirt was thrown on! I loved it that much.

So we began to put our heads together. When I was studying counseling, I was taught how to run an assessment—a tool used in gauging a client's temperament. Before I was credentialed I had to have my assessment run, and later I ran Walt's. Those assessments showed me what a good job eHarmony had done when they had matched us up! Walt and I have the same score in *Control*—which is our willingness to make decisions and to accept responsibility for ourselves and others. We're also both highly independent and self-motivated, have a tendency to see the whole picture, and are able work out details and problems. We're also both firstborns, which can be a problem, because when one of us says, "My way," the other says, "No, my way!" However in this case we came up with "our way"—which we thought would be the perfect solution. I would hold the fort down in South Carolina and get my practice launched while Walt did the nine-month stint in Ohio. It was settled.

GOD'S PLAN

After looking into the requirements in my new home state, I learned that I was going to need to set up my practice a little differently. God and I had a talk about it. I actually argued with Him at first. When I had entered the counseling profession, I had assumed I was there for a reason—I had survived a painful divorce and I was sure my purpose was to help guide other people through that process. But I sensed that God had other ideas. It felt like He was leading me to work primarily with Christian couples who had lost trust in each other and were trying to *avoid* divorce. Working with couples is challenging. You have two personalities to contend with, which takes a lot of skill. To succeed, you'd better have structure, a plan, and the willingness to not give up. God was asking me to go to the front line of the battlefield for marriage.

And He was right, of course. I did have the passion to fight for marriage. After all, I didn't get that kind of help when I needed it the most, and from my own life and through working with others I am convinced that with the right tools it is easier to rebuild a brand new marriage with the same spouse than it is to navigate the challenges of a divorce, especially when children are involved. I believe that.

So I trusted God's marching orders for me (after a little bit of back-and-forth!). By this time I had received a lot of practice-building coaching, which enabled me to enjoy the success I had experienced in Florida. Part of what I had learned was the importance of strategically naming my practice. I researched the area and came up with The Beaufort Center for Marriage.

Then I took the leap of faith. I called our realtor to let her know I wanted to find the perfect home for The Beaufort Center for Marriage and booked a flight to South Carolina. A friend from North Carolina drove down and picked me up at the Charleston airport. We planned a fun girls' weekend in addition to hunting for office space. I had already envisioned the perfect space in my head— glass front doors; beautiful office space; discreet and confidential.

We met the realtor, and after the second space she showed us I needed to look no further. I had found it! It was just like I had envisioned. We entered on the ground floor through the glass double doors. The lobby was tastefully furnished. We took an elevator to the second floor and the office I was shown was basically brand new, with a view of a moss-draped oak tree. The second I walked in I began placing my office furniture in my head, which was a good sign! There was a receptionist to take calls, a break room, a conference room, and a seminar room—everything I needed.

I signed the lease that day, months before my first client would walk through the door. But I wasn't worried. I had the confidence that if I had built a successful practice once, I could do it a second time.

So everything was set. I was ready for the next phase of my life. And three months later, Walt and I said good-bye to Florida.

HOME AT LAST

After a ten-hour drive, we finally arrived at our new home. In the beginning it was a lot like camping out. By this time we were used to waiting for our household goods to arrive, so we bought just enough flatware, silverware, stemware, pots, and pans to get us through. We slept on air mattresses. It was an adventure.

And then the moving van finally arrived. It was like Christmas! All of our earthly possessions were crammed into that tractor-trailer, including boxes from every move. There was stuff from Massachusetts, Kwajalein, Maryland, and Florida. It took the movers eight hours to get the van unloaded.

Then they were gone. And Walt and I were left staring at the 145 boxes that we would have to go through. We felt like ants. We spent our days moving boxes from one spot to another. It took us a solid month just to get them all opened. We worked like Trojans.

During our breaks from the massive job of getting settled, we explored our new hometown. We went on a carriage ride through historic Beaufort, walked the riverfront, took our boat out on the water, and enjoyed beach days at Hunting Island. We began to visit all the restaurants looking for our special date-night spot.

And I didn't just have a new home to move into; there was also a new office to deal with. Walt and I moved my office furniture in and I started decorating. I wanted the space to have a certain feel. I wanted it to feel warm, inviting, and inspirational—not at all stuffy. More like a cozy sitting room—a welcoming, safe place for my clients. The colors were soft aqua and brown. I found scripture wall art that let my clients know they were in the right place. My office was everything I had dreamed it to be. My life was shaping up to be everything I had dreamed it to be. Until June came—much too quickly—and Walt had to report to his new job.

THE SEPARATION

Another long twelve-hour drive. This time we headed north to Port Clinton, Ohio, which is located on the shore of Lake Erie. But this time I wouldn't be staying for long. I had a one-way airline ticket back home.

When we arrived I dropped Walt off at work and set about my task of finding a furnished apartment for him. I didn't have to look far. I asked about apartments at the front desk of the hotel we were staying at, and the clerk happened to know someone who had an apartment for rent on the water. We took one look and signed the lease.

I stayed with Walt for almost a month before heading back to South Carolina. But as the days ticked down, and the day I was supposed to leave drew closer, I started second-guessing our decision. I knew I didn't want to be stuck in that tiny apartment all day by myself during the cold winter—I wouldn't even have a car in Ohio! But I didn't want to leave Walt either.

I didn't realize it at first, but even though I was still with Walt, I was actively grieving the pending loss. The last time we went food shopping together, I didn't push the cart with him; instead I found myself wandering off to other aisles, crying! We had never been separated before, and we're the type of couple who holds hands— even if it's just while walking around inside the grocery store. I couldn't get the thought out of my head... I was leaving my husband. I would be doing everything by myself. I would be shopping, sleeping, eating, and working by myself. I would leave an empty house and return to an empty house. I would be living in a new hometown where I knew no one except the realtor. I got really quiet. And then my frustration turned inward. Walt was worried about me. He had never really seen me like that.

So we looked at our options. We talked about my staying in Ohio, but we both knew it was not God's perfect plan. Finally we decided to work through it. We had dates set on the calendar when we would see each other. And eventually I was able to work through my grief and finally reach the acceptance phase. I realized that as long as God was with me, I would be okay.

Eventually the day came. We said our good-byes at the airport. I boarded the plane and flew back to our new home, alone. When the plane landed, my driver was holding up a sign so I could find him. I grabbed my bag off the carousel and prepared for the forty-five-minute drive home.

I unlocked the door to our house. It was quiet. The first thing I did was call Walt.

Our separation was hard, but it also inspired us. We became very creative during those long months. My favorite time of the day was when the mailman arrived, because chances were good there would be some sort of surprise inside the mailbox. We sent each other greeting cards weekly. Sometimes we would surprise each other with a package.

Second to God, I credit technology for helping us survive our separation—specifically the miraculous invention of the video call. Every night we set up a video call and ate dinner together. On the weekends we would choose a movie to watch on Netflix, make our call, and watch it together. We even celebrated our birthdays over video calls. We decorated our respective homes with balloons and streamers, bought cupcakes to eat together, blew out candles, sang the Happy Birthday song, and watched each other open cards and presents.

Of course, our entire relationship wasn't virtual. There were still times when we flew back and forth and visited each other, just like we had in the old days. And slowly we watched the months go by.

Our separation taught us both one important lesson: We never, ever wanted to be separated again! So while he waited for his assignment to end, Walt decided to take action to make sure we never had to be apart. In the past he had taken some seminary courses in counseling, and after his divorce he ran groups to help people get through their own divorces. Now he decided he would dedicate his spare time to getting the training he needed to join my practice as a board certified Christian life coach. His specialty would be saving marriages.

I was excited about the prospect of my husband coming on board to work with me. Not only would we get to be together, he would also be a real help to my practice. Working with couples, there were so many times I could have used a man's point of view. Now I would finally have one! Which was good news, because calls were coming in to The Beaufort Center for Marriage. Once again my schedule was getting full.

FROM COUNSELOR TO COACH

My clients were primarily people struggling through relation-ship difficulties as opposed to people suffering from mental health disorders. As I worked with them, I found myself moving beyond the boundaries of typical therapy. I was coaching my clients—help-ing them stay focused spiritually, encouraging them, motivating them, and holding them accountable for completing the activities I assigned them.

I began to transform from a traditional counselor to a coach. I knew it was another part of God's plan. I could help more people and save more marriages no matter where a couple was located. As my practice grew, I noticed that when a couple called me for help, they usually fell into one of three categories:

1. They were miserable in their marriage but prepared to make changes.
2. There was no emotional connection in the marriage and the spouse who had not contacted me was unwilling to change.
3. A serious marital betrayal like infidelity had occurred.

The couples I now work with are usually Christian and looking for a Christian way to heal their marriage. This is especially signifi-cant to me, because beginning with my own divorce and through my years working in the field, I couldn't help but notice what I see as a problem with some of the marital advice that gets dispensed in Christian circles: advice sometimes causes more pain than it alle-viates. And that, in my opinion, is the last thing struggling cou-ples need!

For example, a lot of the time the spouse who is trying to work on the marriage and make things better is sent the message that the problem is their fault. For example:

- If they only loved their spouse unconditionally, their spouse would change.

- If they would just obey scripture and have more faith, things would change.
- They just needed to pray harder!
- They should simply forgive and forget and stop nagging their spouse about changing.

And if they didn't do these things, they would get the blame when their marriage didn't get better.

The problem is, whether there is a pattern of alcohol or drug abuse; adultery; pornography; verbal, physical, or emotional abuse; or financial betrayal, there will be a traumatic effect on the marriage. If the spouse who is sinning is not confronted, the marriage will not heal and will eventually die. On the other hand, confronting a sinning spouse can be a terrifying prospect. What if the spouse retaliates, or even worse, simply leaves?

Matthew 18, verses 15 through 17 clearly state to go to your spouse privately, warn them of the consequences of their sin, and then, if they refuse to listen, take two or more others with you to talk to your spouse. If your spouse still won't listen, take the matter to your pastor.

If your pastor can't get your spouse to change, that's the point where it may be necessary to initiate a therapeutic separation in order to seek God's direction. That's where my approach begins. It is scriptural and affords couples the greatest chance for saving their marriage, whether there has been a major betrayal or the problem is just general unhappiness.

During the initial assessment phase, I educate couples about their God-given temperament based on Psalm 139, verses 14 through 18. All individuals have unique temperament strengths as well as areas in which they need to grow. I show my clients that when their God-given temperament needs are not being met, it affects their marriage. And, because I am naturally a peacemaker, my clients tell me that I am able to translate this information to them in an understandable way.

Through this process my clients are able to understand the reasons why their marriage is suffering. They learn which specific needs are not being met, and see how this is affecting their relationship. The best part is that once they understand where their issues come from they are able to show empathy for each other and are motivated to change.

Once they've found that motivation, it's easy to get them to start working on those changes. We look at some of the specific mistakes each partner is making and create a plan for correcting them. Then we have them incorporate some new, positive behaviors that are loving. And because every couple needs to have fun together, we also schedule a weekly date night. It's certainly worked for me and Walt!

Over the years I've learned that healthy communication and conflict resolution are not inborn skills—they must be taught. Most couples do not know the rules for fighting, so I teach them how to fight constructively, not destructively. When couples are able to resolve conflict, it increases intimacy, which is one of the main pathways to passion.

I also ask the couples who work with me to look back at their past. Just as a football coach reviews tapes from a past game to see what didn't work, by looking at their past couples can see if some of their old patterns are sneaking into their marriage and causing problems. This assignment is often met with fear and resistance; people want to leave the past in the past. But there are good, solid reasons to revisit the past. More times than not, when a husband or wife hears about their partner's past pain, often for first time, there is a shift in their relationship. Their empathy builds an intimate connection. This is very transformational.

I also teach my couples how to release their past pain through forgiveness. When a couple is able to grant forgiveness and receive forgiveness, a new level of trust is built. A healthy foundation is laid for a brand new marriage.

TOGETHER AGAIN

My marriage was about to become brand new again, too, because finally those long nine months had passed. We booked my last flight to Ohio. We were bringing Walt home. Our plan, with God's help, went just the way we had hoped.

Around the same time, the office manager at my office told me about a new suite that was opening that might work for me. Since my practice was growing, and Walt would soon need his own space, we went to take a look, and the space was perfect. There were offices located off a private corridor offering even more confidentially.

Today Walt and I are working together out of that new, even-more-perfect office space, and our practice is growing to fill it. And we're planning to add additional associates.

We are also creating a new program that will enable couples to work with us in a more concentrated way. It's what we call Christian Couples Retreat, designed for couples who want to reconnect relationally, emotionally, and spiritually, and energize their marriage. The retreats afford couples something that's hard to find in our busy lives—time to focus solely on each other, away from distractions.

Part of the retreat time is spent in sessions in which we ensure all the nuts and bolts of the marriage are secure. But there is also time for fun, including an opportunity to select from a variety of excursions at the retreat destination. This is an important part of the process. We've designed the retreats to not only jumpstart strengthening the marriage, but also create positive memories. We feel it's an incredible opportunity for couples to enhance and energize their marriages. And it's the latest exciting step in what God has planned for us.

CONCLUSION

• • • • • • • •

LOOKING FORWARD

"Behold, I stand at the door and knock; if anyone hears My voice
and opens the door, I will come in to him and dine with him
and he with me."

—Revelation 3:20

SO WHAT HAVE I learned through this incredible journey? The biggest lesson lies in those words James spoke to me so many years ago when my marriage was crumbling, and unable to bear the pain any longer, I was, too.

"Just trust Him."

I've learned that try as we might, we really have no control over what our loved ones choose to do. There is nothing we can do to persuade someone to love us, even if that person has promised to stand by our side until death. I never ever imagined that my marriage would end, and I did everything I knew to try to save it. But it was not my choice to make. However, when it felt like everything had been lost, I truly learned that I was not alone. I learned firsthand that God always has our highest good in mind.

By trusting God I was able to not only get through my heartache, but also accomplish things I never could have imagined. There was a time when I thought my purpose was primarily to be a mother and a wife. But God clearly had plans prepared in advance for me. I never imagined I would pursue a Ph.D. and eventually own a practice doing what I love. Yet by trusting God and following His lead, I found a tremendous amount of fulfillment and joy.

God has brought me a marriage to a man I love and who loves and honors me. God has enabled me to help change people's lives, improve and save people's marriages, and do some real good in the world.

My prayer is that by reading this book and seeing what God has done for me, you will see that God also wants to transform and heal your heart from the wounds of your past, especially if the people who were supposed to love you failed to do so. More than anyone, I've written this book for you.

I want you to understand that God loves you and to know that by growing in your trust in Him, He will fulfill all your God-given desires, goals, and dreams. It doesn't matter what people say you can or cannot do. I was told that I would not be able to accomplish a lot of things. There was a time when I couldn't see where my life was headed, had no idea where I would end up, and had no vision of how fulfilling my life would become. But God knew.

I believe that the secret to changing your future is to change your thinking—about yourself and about God. When you surrender your life to God, He gives you a vision for your life, and you must have the courage to fulfill it. Yes, there may be pain—but the pain you go through is how He shapes you for His purposes. Something good can come out of the pain. You might even be able to use it to help others make changes in their own lives. The day will come when it will all make sense and you will thank Him, because the pain can be a gift.

No matter what you might have in mind for yourself, God's plan for your life will not be altered. It is what sets you apart so you can make a difference in other people's lives. I have shared my own personal story so you can understand that I empathize with your suffering. You can trust me to offer the understanding, love, and compassion you need to get to the other side. A new life is awaiting you.

I have no idea what God has in store for me next. As far as my career as a marriage coach and counselor goes, I know that I will be waiting for the next person God sends through my door or who connects with me online. In my personal life I'm looking forward to creating even more family memories and togetherness. I plan on more travels with my beloved Walt, and I do hope God decides to send a couple more daughters-in-law to the family (I need more girls!), and grandchildren.

It has been thirty-two years since I clearly heard God's voice and invited Him to come into my life. I was looking for a love that would never let me go. That decision was the greatest act of trust I have ever given to anyone. I believed Him when He said He loved me. And in doing so, His love enveloped me.

Through those dark moments when my mother left, my father took his life, and my husband betrayed me, I learned to trust Him. Even when God said no, I trusted that His plan for my life would be accomplished. Through various trials I learned that His love is unending. And because of His love I learned that no matter the circumstances, He is strong enough to carry me through.

Trust and love go hand in hand. I can honestly say that I trust and love Him more because of the trials that have been permitted in my life. My journey has deepened my compassion for others, given me the understanding to help others turn their lives around, and kept me true to the one voice that has faithfully led me.

My faith continues to grow deeper because I know that wherever I go God is beside me, His voice—the Holy Spirit—is within me, and Christ—His Son—prays for me.

Of course I have experienced difficult times. But I wouldn't be the person I am today if my life had been painless. If you are carrying hidden pain because your heart has been broken by unrequited love, I want you to know that there is someone who will love you to no end. God is faithful and trustworthy. He desires your highest good. He is not like any other. He is true to His promises.

Maybe this is the reason you are reading *Enveloped*. You want to trust God, but you have been hurt so deeply by others that you are afraid to trust Him. You hear His voice calling you to Him and you want to give yourself to Him, but you are holding back. If you are that person, I understand. You feel vulnerable. And you need someone who understands your struggles. Someone you can be authentic with and feel safe.

My experience has taught me that safe people are those who accept, understand, and love me. They are gentle with my feelings. They don't judge me. They really listen, give advice when asked, and encourage me. They offer me a soft shoulder to cry on when I need it.

God is like that. He always does the right thing. He acts with fairness and longs for your highest good—and makes sure your plans achieve those ends.

Time and time again I have seen that we have great worth and significance to God. His love is everlasting. He will never leave us or forsake us. When we believe God, trust Him, and receive His unending love, He gives us everything we need. He has a plan and a purpose for our lives.

No matter what is happening in your life, trust in God. He will meet those hidden needs you have that no person can totally fulfill. Take that step of faith. Believe that God will show you His plan for your life in a personal way.

He did it for me. He will do it for you.

THE LORD'S
UNENDING LOVE

OR THOSE OF you who have endured betrayal and loss, the most important message I can leave with you is that there is someone who loves with a love that will never let you go. The Lord Christ longs to draw you close and show you a love you have never known. He has been pursuing you for years. He wants you to find your significance, security, and love in Him so that you can live the life He has planned for you right now for all eternity.

Christ wants you to trust His love. It is a gift. Here is how you receive His love and begin a relationship with Him: Admit you made mistakes. So have I. For that matter everyone has. Our mistakes separate us from God. God says, "All have sinned and fall short of the glory of God" (Romans 3:23).

God loves you so much that he sent Jesus to pay for your mistakes—your sin. Jesus is asking you to accept this gift of grace. "For the wages of sin is death, but the free gift of God is eternal life in Christ Jesus our Lord" (Romans 6:2).

To believe in Jesus and become a Christian you simply agree and accept by faith that Christ died for your sin according to the scriptures, that He was buried, and that He was raised on the third day according to the scriptures (1 Corinthians 15:3–4).

The moment you decide to believe in your heart and receive His gracious love, you receive the Holy Spirit. He will never leave you or forsake you. All your sins are forgiven. You are given a brand new life. And when your life ends you will make your home in heaven—with Him.

Repeat this prayer if you are ready to receive His unending love:

Kind Father,

For the first time I finally realize that Jesus truly loves me and that He died for all my mistakes—all my sins. Today I want to receive His gift of grace and I accept Christ as my Savior and Lord. Jesus, I believe You are who You say You are. You are God. I am Yours. You are mine. I am giving my life to You and right now receive Your unending love.

In Jesus's name,
Amen

ABOUT THE AUTHOR

CAROL ERB IS founder and director of The Beaufort Center for Marriage, LLC, a Christian counseling and marriage coaching center in Beaufort, South Carolina. Carol specializes in helping Christian couples move past a rough spot in their marriage and avoid divorce.

After earning a BS in recreation therapy from East Carolina University, Carol worked as a recreation therapist at a psychiatric hospital, provided music therapy at Cumberland County Mental Health, and then became a stay-at-home mom devoting the next fifteen years to serving her husband and children. She continued her education and received her master's in Christian counseling from Southeastern Seminary followed by earning her Ph.D. in clinical Christian counseling from Cornerstone University. Her professional background in mental health includes working as a rehabilitation counselor for NC Services for the Blind and as a therapy coordinator for a geriatric/psychology unit at Quincy Medical Center—the teaching hospital of Boston College, and she created a school-based mental health program for Ebeye, Marshall Islands. She owned a Christian counseling practice in Key Largo, Florida, prior to her practice in Beaufort, South Carolina.

Carol is a board certified Christian counselor and marriage coach providing individual and couples sessions, marriage intensives, seminars, and destination retreats. An inspirational speaker, she travels the southeast speaking for Christian Women's Connection of Stonecroft Ministries and writes bi-monthly feature articles for her website blog.

Carol is an active member of the Beaufort Chamber of Commerce and a member of the American Association of Christian Counseling, the National Association of Christian Counselors, and the International Christian Coaching Association. In 2008 she received the Kwajalein Range Services Presidential Award for service to the Marshallese people and in 2013 she was awarded Servant Leadership Award finalist by the Board of Christian Professional and Pastoral Counselors for the American Association of Christian Counselors.

Carol Erb lives with her husband, Walt, in Beaufort, South Carolina—America's happiest seaside town.

CONNECT WITH CAROL

. • • • • • .

On the Web:

drcarolerb.com
beaufortmarriage.com

Through Social Media:

twitter.com/carolerb
facebook.com/drcarolerb
pinterest.com/drcarolerb/

For Speaking Opportunities:

hello@drcarolerb.com

Keep in touch with *Enveloped*:

envelopedbook.com
facebook.com/envelopedbook

Made in the USA
Charleston, SC
20 June 2015